I0176248

Russian Ripped

ILYA SULIMA

Copyright © 2012 Ilya Sulima. All rights reserved. No part of this book may be used or reproduced in any manner whatsoever without the authors written permission.

ISBN: 0615693598
ISBN-13: 9780615693590

Dedicated to everyone who gets up just one more time than they fall

NOTICE

Be sure to check with your doctor and have full clearance prior to training or committing to any workout/training program. Not all training programs fit all individuals. The author and his affiliates do not take any responsibility for any injuries or deaths that may occur in any physical training program. The information in this book is written for entertainment and knowledge purposes only. Any individual following any program or programs from Russian Ripped does so at his/her own risk after being released by a doctor to do so.

	Acknowledgments	i
1	The Comrade Attitude	1
2	Breaking the Vicious Circle of Fitness Restarts	10
3	Follow the Mirror Comrade, Not The Scale!	21
4	I've been going to the gym and I'm still struggling to lose weight. Why?	25
5	The Comrade Food	35
6	General Comrade Supplements	75
7	Gym Etiquette and Other Important Considerations	82
8	Basic in Gym Stretches and Training Philosophies	89
9	Mighty Chest Basics	104
10	Mighty Back	137

11 Mighty Legs   163

12 Mighty Arms   182

13 Mighty Shoulders   201

14 Awesomeness Glorious Abbs   215

15 Run Comrade Run!   223

16 Combo It Up Comrade!   231

17 The 6 Step Plan to Victory!   242

18 The Renegade Soviet Special Forces Training Option   261

19 The Bear, Wolf, Rabbit, Beaver Connection   291

20 Words of Glorious Wisdom   296

ACKNOWLEDGMENTS

I would like to thank everyone who helped me with this book. I would especially like to thank Joe, Patrick, Rick, Scott and Roger.

Chapter 1 - The Comrade Attitude

You know Comrade, before I was a Major in the Soviet Russian Red Army, I was an unqualified conscript. I was a no good private in the glorious Red Army, and I was not fully accepted by the strong and the ripped average Soviet peoples. Then one day, I understood the secrets of what it actually takes to get Russian Ripped!

Ok Comrade, I will be honest with you, it took longer than one day, but the main thing is that I took the first step towards change. That first step to becoming Russian Ripped was having the right attitude.

When a Comrade has the wrong attitude towards a fitness goal, motivation is low. With low motivation the saboteur of goal achievement never rests. My attitude before I started training was so bad that one American infantry division could have wiped out the entire Russian Army. That was what my motivation was like. Low!

But when I got Russian Ripped after changing my attitude, I alone was able to fight off twenty American soldiers, three hundred Spartans, five alligators and a hungry bear all at the same time. I did all this while holding a handsome girl in one hand and brushing the glorious abbs with the other hand. The reflection of the sunlight bounced off the magnificent abbs and blinded the enemies.

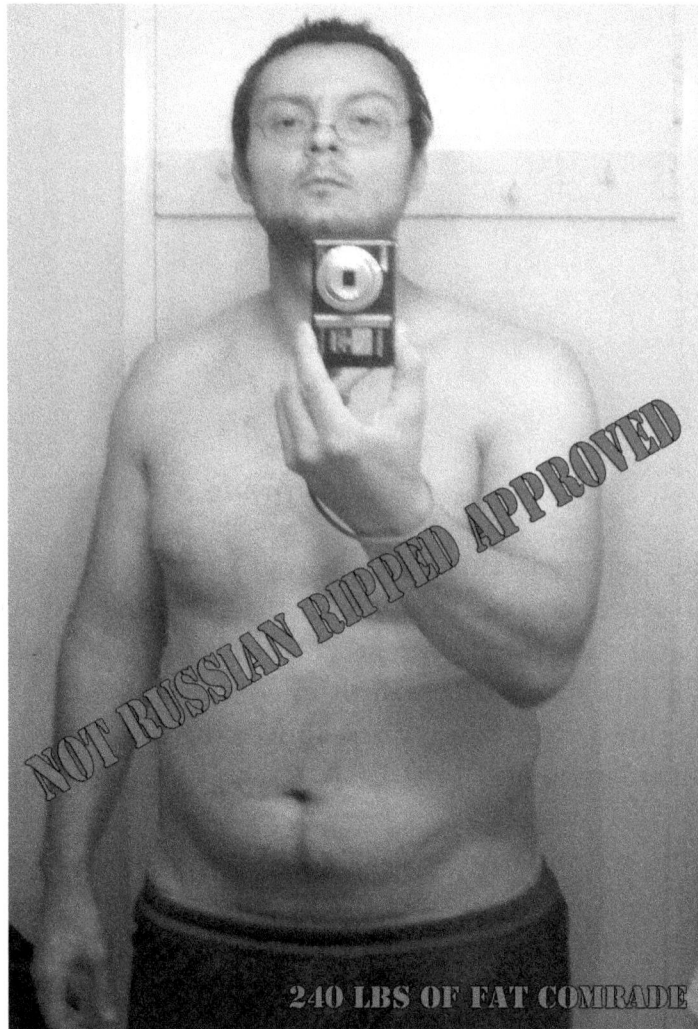

Take a close look at me when I was 240lbs Comrade. The way I looked then was also the way I felt, bad. Every day I got up, looked at my self in the mirror and then went to work. How you name it, it was 9-5 job and slowly I slipped so far that eventually came drinking vodka time, and then came the drinking friends, and then I did not want to do anything. My thinking was set up for failure, not just in the realm of fitness but towards life overall. How you say, the way you think is the way you act and the way you act is the person you are. I was a fat @$$ who did not accept responsibility for his health. So, I asked myself some questions.

1.   Are you happy getting up in the morning and looking at the mirror Comrade? Or do you not even see yourself anymore?
2.   Did you become Mr. Six Pack or did you fall in love with the couch?
3.   Are you where you want to be?

I answered all those questions with a No, or how we say it back home (NIET). Then, I decided to take the time to evaluate some of the things wrong with me.

Joint pain in the knees? **Yes**
Sluggish over all feeling? **Yes**
Lazy sleepiness after eating? **Yes**
Shortness of breath when moving fast? **Yes**
Lower back pain? **Yes**
Positive and full of energy? **No**
Dull autopilot zombie like feeling most of the day? **Yes**

Well, long story short Comrade it came to a point where positive change needed to happen. Sweating while just sitting on my @$$ without any movement behind a desk made me think carefully about how I got to that point. I had enough; I got up, walked up to the bathroom mirror, pointed at myself and said.

"You stupid fat idiot, wake up! Is this the glorious life you want for yourself? How dare you not blend in with Comrades who are in Russian Ripped shape? Look at them all, they are so fit, they have so much energy and they are always so positive. Don't you want to be like that? You are no worse than any of them. You have the potential to feel and look fantastic, but instead you waste time on irrelevant stuff like watching boot leg "I Love Lucy" reruns. Don't you think it's time to do something about your current situation for good?"

After answering yes, (DA) to the last question I went down to a secret KGB storage vault located under the Moscow subway where the Soviet secret experiments went on with the aliens. I was lucky because my uncle Dima worked there. So, after slipping my uncle three bottles of vodka that bastard finally allowed me to go through the secret door where I found the recipe for success. It was there I found a file that was called Attitude/ Step - 1. Here, is a stolen translated copy just for you.

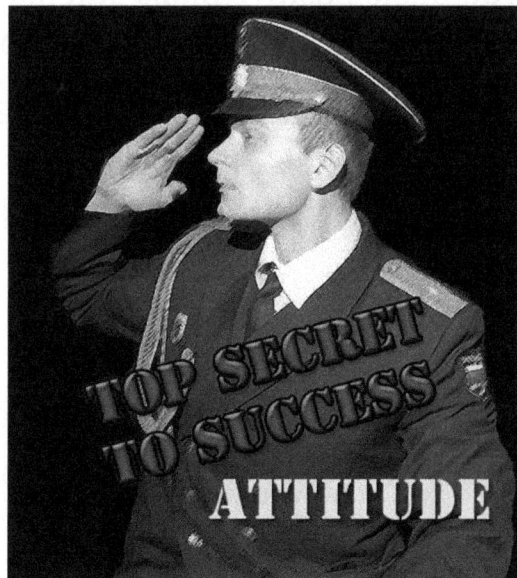

(Attitude/Step - 1)

Hello Comrade, please keep in mind that the information in this document is essential for success in order to achieve what ever it is you wish to set your mind on. Utilize and reference this short document as often as necessary.

Attitude

Attitude is a key part of the equation to success. Before a Comrade knows what it is that he or she wants to do in life, attitude already sets the mood and pushes the Comrade in the direction of that dominating mood.

It's not some magical life circumstances that move us forward towards an uncharted direction Comrades. It's the attitude with which we face these circumstances and how we react/respond based on the dominant attitude present at the moment of the reaction.

Do you make an effort to assure yourself that you have the ability to achieve your dreams on a daily basis Comrade?
Do you believe in your self Comrade?
Do you encourage others or bring them down Comrade?

If you did not respond positively to all the questions above, take the time to think about why that is without pointing the finger at someone else to shift responsibility.......
As you read the next part, please pause for a second after each line.

Say your name.. **You are a winner**
Say your name.. **You are strong**
Say your name.. You **are motivated**
Say your name.. **You are positive**
Say your name.. **You are organized**
Say your name.. **You make positive plans and fall through on them**
Say your name.. **You take responsibility for your actions**

Now say these things out loud to yourself in a convincing voice standing in front of a mirror. What have you to be afraid of? This is your life. Do not be afraid to improve your life. Do not procrastinate to have the right attitude now. If you can, stop what ever it is you are doing, go up to a mirror, point at your self and say these things to yourself out loud. Do it! Not doing it shows you are not serious.

...You are a winner
...You are strong
...You are motivated
...You are positive
...You are organized

…You make positive plans and fall through on them
…You take responsibility for your actions

Repetition of positive thoughts every day elevates the way we feel and directly impacts our attitude. We will always have problems in life regardless of where or who we are. The only thing we can do is face these problems. How we face these problems sets off a sequence of events that may be dealt with in the positive or in the negative. To someone a flat car tire may have ruined the whole day. A whole day lost because the individual faced a basic problem with the wrong attitude and did not let it go. Do not dwell on the little things… not worth it.

When negativity builds inside a Comrade, eventually it needs to be released. Have you ever been on the receiving end of someone's destructive energy release because he or she had a lousy day? This is an excellent example of why positive attitude is so important. No one wants to be on the receiving end of negativity. But, if the Comrade has a positive attitude, negativity doesn't stand a chance.

Negative attitude = **Stress**

Stress = Health problems

Stress = Pushes away others

Stress = Influences unfavorable decisions

Stress = Ruins normal homeostasis balance of life

So Comrade, every morning you get up, motivate yourself with repeated positive sayings for a few minutes and add more constructive suggestions to the list if you like. Believe the positive things that you say while looking in the mirror and say these things with confidence and strength. Attitude will be elevated significantly by the time you finish. Blood will be pumping through the body faster than normal, and a sense of confidence will arise. The day will emerge better than average even if something unpleasant happens. Why? Because through positive attitude you take control of how outside influences affect you. Think of positive attitude as an invisible shield that is always with you. The purpose of this shield is to have negativity bounce off.

Positive attitude = lessens stress

Positive attitude = Makes a Comrade more approachable

Positive attitude = Makes a Comrade more likable

Positive attitude = Helps focus on goals

Positive attitude = Gets $!# done!

For a moment let's say that you need to get in shape. Do you honestly think that wishing and training a few times will change your physique? It's pretty obvious that getting in shape takes time and effort. It also takes consistency and willpower. Willpower is influenced by attitude.

If you get off work at 5pm and you worked the whole day with a negative attitude, will you step into the gym and give it your best? Or will you just avoid the gym, go home and continue on in a negative mood causing more negativity to build and brew around you? You see Comrade, attitude among many other things also influences choices. These choices many times we do not even think of. We just react. We react with the attitude dominating our thoughts at that particular moment in time.

Here, are two examples of attitude based reactions and outcomes.

Boris wanted to go for a run after work with his friends. Unfortunately, the tractor he was fixing had serious problems. The whole day Boris ran into unexpected problems. He was nagging about it on and on without realizing that bitterness took over him entirely by the time he got off work. Boris did not go for a run with his friends. Instead, he went home, got in a fight with his wife who also had a long day at work and yelled at his son for no good reason (negative energy release). Never once did Boris realize that he was not in control of himself. This is a sad story that parallels life in many more ways than one. Most likely Boris will not be known as a respectable citizen who loves his family. He will probably be remembered as someone who likes to yell at his wife and son.

Peter came to fill in for Boris the following day because Boris made a decision not show up for work. Peter wanted to go to the gym after finishing the tractor repairs and so he told himself that nothing was going to get in his way. He had a devilishly difficult time that day, but he took on all situations that came along one by one and certainly did not dwell on them. Then, when the work day came to an end, Peter went to the gym and had a fantastic workout. After the gym, Peter came home tired but happy and accomplished. His wife Svetlana who came home just a few minutes before he did was also tired after teaching a class of rowdy young kids the whole day. But because Peter was in a pleasant mood he offered to help around the house and then he even prepared dinner. Svetlana realized how lucky she was to have such a marvellous husband, and she also became charged with a positive attitude. After dinner, Peter helped his two kids with their homework and encouraged them to study hard.

Peter has chosen the right attitude and caused positive chain reactions all around. Through his actions people will find out good things about him. People will know that Peter is a loving caring father and husband.

On the Comradometer scale of (1 to 10) if one is a Boris and ten is a Peter, which do you fall closer to in the past six months? Does attitude have anything to do with it? If you fall closer to a Boris, it might be a good idea to start taking responsibility.

THE COMRADOMETER SCALE ©

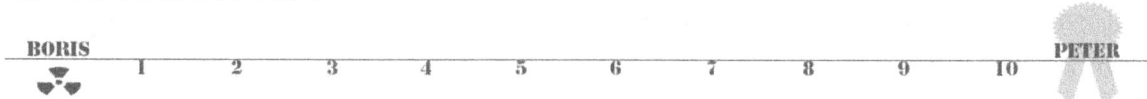

| BORIS | 1 | 2 | 3 | 4 | 5 | 6 | 7 | 8 | 9 | 10 | PETER |

Another Positive secret strategy to improve attitude is this:

Pretend that you are an immensely important General or CEO who is looked up to and is admired by many. Because of this you must maintain a positive outlook on life and show strength. However to do this all the time is difficult so you need help. And who is going to support this important General/CEO? The answer is you. When dealing with a tough situation, especially if you are caught off guard, step outside your body for a second. Look at yourself and advise yourself to act like a person of courage and integrity committing to virtuous actions. Tell yourself to follow through on significant commitments and tell yourself why you think you need to act with honourable intentions. So you see, you become your own positive personal advisor and improve how you feel by advising yourself outside yourself. You build yourself up in moments of instability. This can be done before an important meeting, or before you go to work out. This technique may be applied in various difficult situations. Try it sometimes. Just don't talk to the imaginary you out loud. That's a possible medical condition, not a self elevation technique.

We are always faced with choices Comrades. The attitude we decide to choose paves the life road that we drive on. Many times it rains and snows on our road, but summer and sunny days always come around. Each one of us has the choice to prolong the summer with the right attitude or turn everything around us into a cold miserable winter at a blink of an eye. Choose the right attitude Comrades! Life is lived better with the sun, not in the snow.

(Step-1 End of file)

Now that I have shared this secret file, I can reflect back and say that if it was not for the right attitude, I would not be happy and in shape Comrade. When I started getting in shape I had no encouragement or support form other Comrades. I was a lone bear in a big forest but every morning I motivated myself to move. Every morning I looked myself dead in the eye at the mirror and said "Today I act to win, today I will become stronger than yesterday, today I am going to stay positive no matter what, today I take responsibility." Then I would go to work, and at lunch time a Comrade food truck would roll up with the salo covered chocolate. (Frozen fat, covered with chocolate on a stick). All the weak Comrades ran to get the free treat provided by the party. At that moment I would step outside myself and ask myself.

"Self, do you want a six pack?"

"Yes"

"Then why the hell are you walking in the wrong direction? Get back on the ball and get ripped, winners go all the way, and you Sir, are a winner."

Now Comrade, will you stay positive even when someone or something is snowing on your parade or will you just choose the easy way out and give up? The way we face grim and enjoyable events is through the dominating attitude at the moment of the event. Then, we act with the attitude foundation at that moment upon that event. Attitude is the driving force of mental atmosphere in which we exist day to day.

...You are a winner
...You are strong
...You are motivated
...You are positive
...You are organized
...You make positive plans and fall through on them
...You take responsibility for your actions

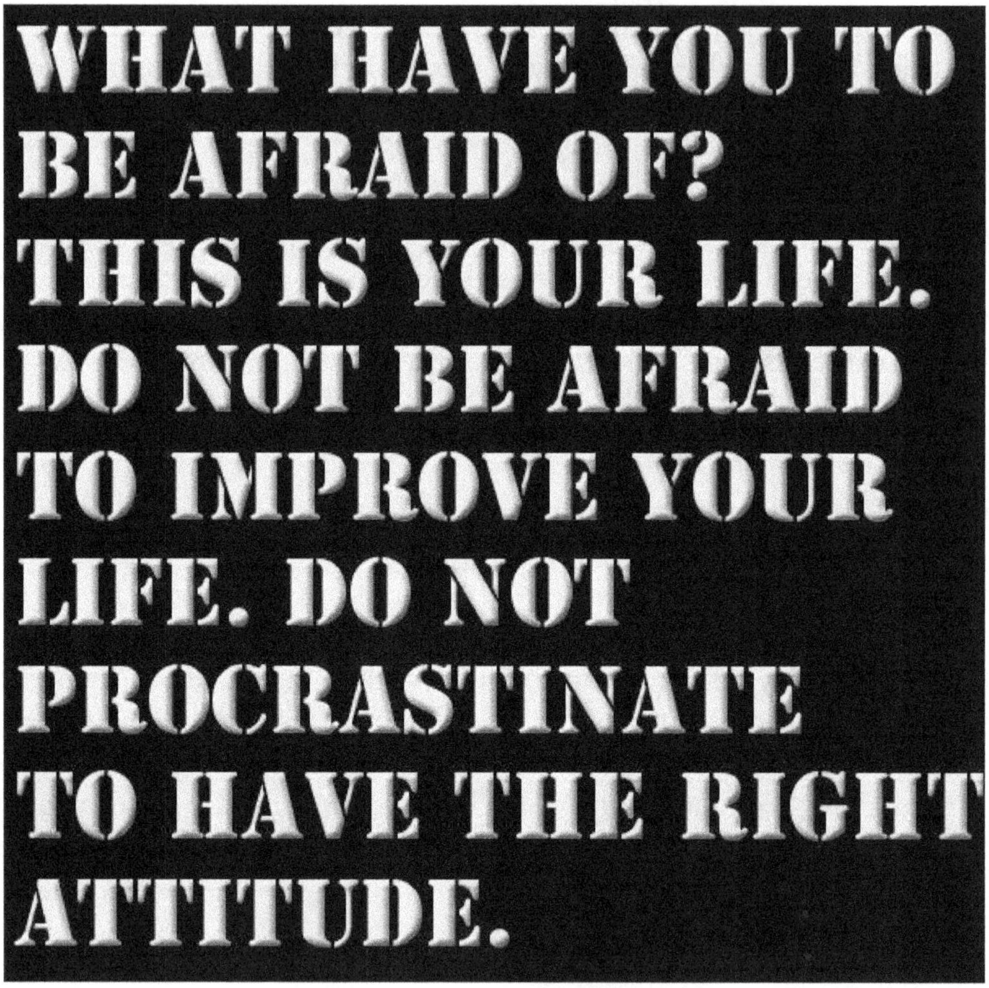

WHAT HAVE YOU TO BE AFRAID OF? THIS IS YOUR LIFE. DO NOT BE AFRAID TO IMPROVE YOUR LIFE. DO NOT PROCRASTINATE TO HAVE THE RIGHT ATTITUDE.

The Successes Formula

(*Positive Attitude*) + (*Belief in Self*) + (*Research*) + (*Action*) + (*Focused Persistence*)

= (Manifestation of Idea/Goal)

When the Success Formula is applied to achieving the Russian Ripped look to a standard Comrade, the following description applies.

• The Comrade is Positive.

• The Comrade believes that he or she has the opportunity to get Russian Ripped regardless of circumstances.

• The Comrade dedicates time to learn the facts about getting in shape and does not follow hearsay.

• The Comrade takes action on the new knowledge.

• The Comrade does not give up and moves forward towards the focused goal/idea on a daily basis until he or she achieves that objective.

Result: The Comrade gets Russian Ripped!

(Note) "No motivational speaker or self improvement technique will work unless you take responsibility for your actions. The good news is, the past is not the present. Take responsibility now to grasp hold of the winning future others only dream of. It's time to act and get in shape. Move!"

Chapter 2 - Breaking the Vicious Circle of Fitness Restarts

Glorious Comrade! In this chapter, I will point out some of the initial pit falls, and when some of these pitfalls happen. If you find yourself in the vicious fitness circle going back and forth, I hope that the positive attitude you have chosen will prevail in times of doubt.

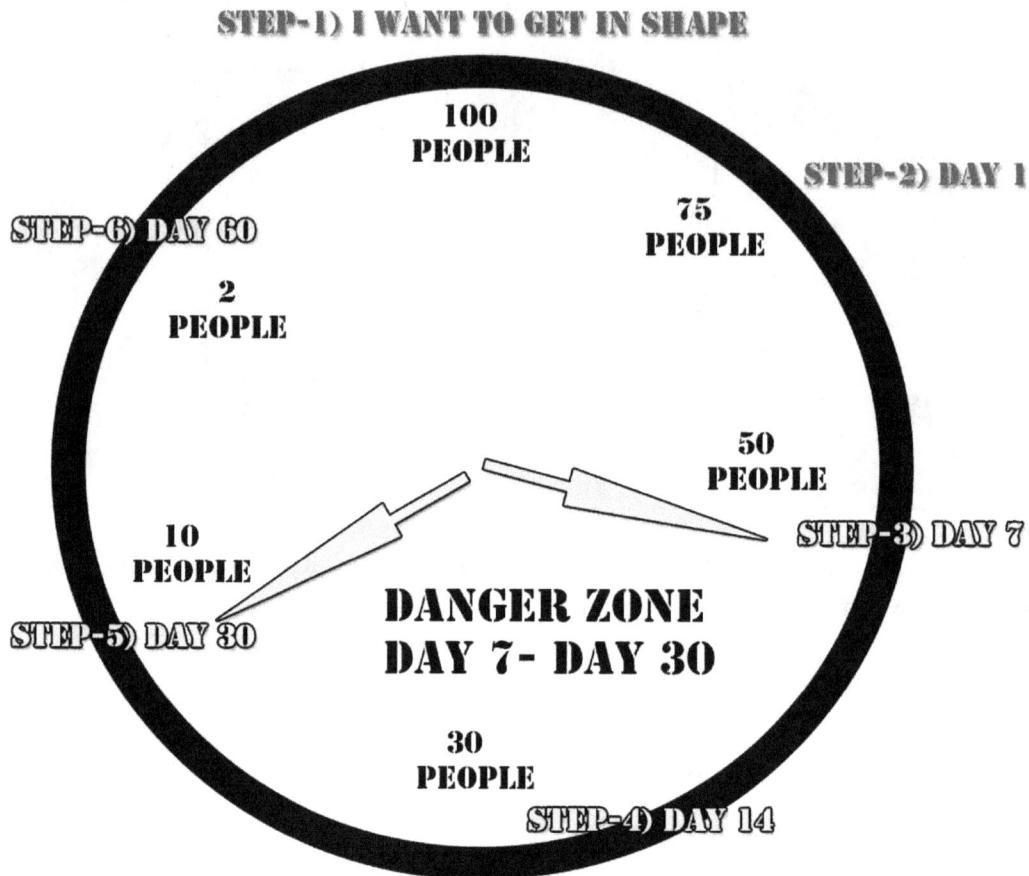

STEP-1) I WANT TO GET IN SHAPE

100 PEOPLE

STEP-2) DAY 1

75 PEOPLE

STEP-6) DAY 60

2 PEOPLE

50 PEOPLE

10 PEOPLE

STEP-3) DAY 7

STEP-5) DAY 30

DANGER ZONE
DAY 7- DAY 30

30 PEOPLE

STEP-4) DAY 14

As you look at the circular diagram above, you will see that there are 100 Comrades who want to get in shape. Unfortunately on just a 60 day starting phase, almost every one of them drops off and at one point or another and falls back to step one. Unfortunately coming back to step one is a particularly common occurrence. We will now go into detail as to why some pit falls occur and what you can do to ensure yourself a better chance of getting through the first 60 days.

Step 1) I want to get in Shape!!!

This is one of the most common steps taken by Comrades. As time progresses into the future, more and more Comrades will face step one, (usually around December time). This is the magical time Comrades are telling themselves that they want to get in shape.

But what does it mean to get in shape?

Did you know that to every person getting in shape means something different? Some Comrades might want to reduce body fat while others might want to have the ability of running a 10K every other day. Both of these examples are different and yet true. Unfortunately, the first pitfall happens here!

In this pitfall, as a Comrade wants to get in shape, he or she thinks in uncertain terms about what he or she might want to look like without significant clue as to what needs to be done. Not identifying a clear fitness goal sets up disaster for the Comrade from the start. However, at this stage, all though no definite plans and no sound structure is present, something else is.

A powerful impulse to act!

This impulse is like a fast acting emotional adrenalin shot that causes the Comrade to change and do something. At that moment, the Comrade is highly vulnerable and open to making many mistakes by acting on that powerful impulse without rational thought. The action that usually happens here is one that satisfies the impulsive desire by means of instant gratification. (Like joining an expensive gym and signing a contract for a year without sufficient contemplation). If you want to become Russian Ripped, later on in the book a complete system is presented just for that. But, if for whatever reason this is not the path a Comrade has chosen, a different sound system must be present to achieve specific goals. This even holds true if you already have experience in the field of fitness. Experience alone without a plan is like a bear who tells other bears that at one point he was fast enough to get the honey and get away from the bees. The bear knows how to get the honey, but in the current state of the present time the bear simply reflects on the past and the past is not the present. The bear does not have the honey now. Without a plan, getting the honey will lead to getting stung by the bees. Even though the bear has experience, without a plan, experience alone is not enough.

What follows next is step two, of which only 75 of the original 100 Comrades follow through on. The drop off happens because many other outside priorities over power the impulse to act; if acting on the impulse does not happen immediately the impulse loses strength and dwindles away.

What to do in step one?

• Read Russian Ripped before taking action on impulse!
• Define clearly what it means to be in shape for you.
• Brainstorm a short term and a long term plan. (Utilize but do not entirely rely on personal trainers or "how to" DVDs).
• Stay realistic and ask what other priorities are present in your life that may prevent you from committing to a long term training program. (Priorities and excuses are not the same thing).
• The more you know before you start training, the better chances you will have in achieving set goals. However, learning as you go is also good hands on experience.
• Stay positive and remember attitude is key!
• Do not spend money on fitness stuff at this stage. New gym clothes are not the answer. Instead, earn new gym clothes by training consistently for a few weeks.
• Do you want to tell the world about the choice you made about getting in shape or do you want to shock everyone? Usually if you don't tell anyone, the compliments will come in on their own in due time, and that's when you'll know you are doing something right.

Step 2) Day 1 to day 7

Congratulations, you just walked into a gym or ran a mile around the house. Now what? Well, this is the hype stage. This intense emotional positive state naturally lasts for a few days or even weeks. During the hype stage, the Comrade is exited about getting in shape and starts some form of training. But something else happens in the hype stage: Onset of pain, soreness, decline in motivation, beginning of inconsistency in training, inconsistency in eating healthy foods and self imbalanced judgment. What is self imbalanced judgment?

(Incorrect judgment of workload to reward ratio)

This is where the Comrade says or thinks something like:
"I can party or eat this, and that, I worked out hard this week, and I deserve it." This is a pitfall because negative behavior is sparked by negative thought.
(Note) The negative thoughts of self pity push the Comrade to act in a negative way. This is so because in this early stage, the foundation of effective training habits is not yet established, the Comrade gives into pain and temptation.
(Note) Eating a pizza and other junk does not justify a successful start week. By day 7, 25 more Comrades fall off the boat leaving half of the original 100 Comrades on track.

What to do in step two?

• Focus on long term results and realize that the first steps are the most difficult to make.

- Do not throw yourself to the wolves right away and train like a mad man. But also don't waste time by just going through exercise motions. Find a medium.
- Start to educate yourself and tell yourself that this is a long term commitment, not a resolution. If it's just a short term band aid why bother with training at all?
- Remind yourself that attitude is key!
- Remind yourself that you have the forward momentum!

Step 3) Day 7 to day 14

Comrades who make it to this point ask themselves what they might change to better the training regimen and yet not take the full fledged steps to educate themselves further.

To want something but not fall through on the want is a common human behavior; especially when physical exercise and effort is involved. The Comrades also begin to feel tiered if they in fact trained hard the first week. This is the stage where pain contemplation presents itself loud and clear through the glorious inner voice.

Thoughts like: "Oh my back is sore, my arms are in pain, I'm tiered, I think I pulled something and I need to stop for a while, yah this is right for me, but it's too much work etc…" start to float around.

One of the biggest dangers is the Friday, Saturday weekend of week 2. If a Comrade party hardy Friday night, sleeps in Saturday and lounges around through Sunday, getting back on the ball Monday when regular life starts again is a 50/50 probability.

That's three whole days lost. Monday morning will be almost like starting all over except without the hype because of potential food bloating or over all sluggish zombie like state that carried on from the weekend. Not to mention that negative habits were strengthened over that weekend as well.

(Note) Reinforcement of negative habit is like constantly telling yourself not to think of the invisible pink elephant in the room. You think of the elephant constantly. What you think of most (example: junk food) you act on.

As wise Yoda from the American cinema would say "Creature of habit man is."

This common scenario takes the Comrade back to step one of the 60 day cycle just 14 days later. This pitfall is called *The Week Two Weekend Derailment.*

What to do in Step Three?

- Focus on a clear training plan.
- By finishing week two strong, you are part of the top 30%.
- Attack the Friday as if it's a Monday.
- You might not realize this, but others start looking up to you at this point and admire the strength you are showing. "If others are complimenting you or try to bring you down that's because you elevated yourself by means of positive action. The action you are taking is causing a reaction that brings out the best and worst in people."

- Realize that you are building a foundation that others wish for, where you are taking the steps to not wish so but do so.
- Life is difficult at times and walls of (emotion and stress) will erect themselves in front of you. There is no reason for you not to jump over those walls or break through them and continue ahead if you are totally focused and committed. If every time something bad happened and this bad thing got in your way derailing you from achieving an objective, would you quit eating food? So why quit training?

(Note) If the voice in your head just automatically replied because food is more important and necessary unlike physical training is, the idea of getting in shape and training at the moment is but a secondary priority to you. Secondary priorities lack intensity and focus. Please come off the autopilot system and adapt the idea of getting in shape from a secondary, to a first priority.

- Making it to week three is an incredible feeling. Do you want to jeopardize that?
- Remind yourself that attitude is key!
- Remind yourself that you have the forward momentum! No one but you is in charge.

Step 4) Day 14 to day 30

Two factors that play significantly in step four are (inconsistencies in nutritious food habits and the natural desire to see immediate cosmetic improvement in the mirror as well as on the scale). Without the mental grip over the two factors; frustration builds up inside most Comrades. In a short amount of time, when the boiling point is reached, frustration evolves in to an all out psychological burnout.

It's highly likely that the average Comrade has never trained so hard before while experiencing the standard work, school, life schedule. Standard established lifestyle habits that do not include a training program after all are hard to break. Usually the combination of physical fatigue mixed in with questions like: "How much longer" and "I did 100 sit ups every day for the past 14 days, where the hell are my abbs?" Sabotage further progress.

"In a state of pain we look for comfort. However, if you feel no pain, do not expect to gain. Pain is part of the process. This pain period is a big factor as to why so many do not progress. They give up. Defeat the pain and you win the body you want."

What to do in Step Four?

- By this time you must have an established organized plan. You must know what you are doing each day of the week in the gym as well as outside the gym.
- Physical pain has probably been peaking for some time but staying positive is crucial. The barrier that breaks numerous Comrades is set here.

- By entering week three you must have an organizational approach to food. Skipping meals or not eating in the morning saps consistent energy output and pushes a Comrade towards a crash come mid day.
- Realize that you may have been conditioned to expect change quickly through out life. When it comes to training, changes will occur, but they will not be instant. Do you truly want to go back to day 1? A few months from now if you quit at this point you will realize you could have been a few months ahead if you didn't stop.
- Remind yourself that attitude is key!

Step 5) Day 30 to day 60

After eating clean food for thirty days and training hard, this is the magic stage of cosmetic change. It's in step five that noticeable changes begin to appear. Also, the old habits of non training begin to break and a new positive training habit begins to form. The down side to this stage is that change happens slowly.

(Note) Comrades who do not have confidence in themselves may break because the change is not fast enough; even though the changes are happening.

This is also a high probability time period for slipping in to the yoyo routine. A loss of self control leading to food binging can viciously take over Comrades in this stage. When this food binge possession happens, it's as if the Comrade is a hungry bear digging through garbage and can not stop eating everything in sight. This sets the Comrade on the perfect yoyo path to train hard and binge. Advance and fall back over and over. The binge incidents are usually triggered when the Comrade for some reason starves him or her self or goes on a low carbohydrate diet.

(Note) DO NOT starve yourself! If someone suggests that you need to go on a low calorie or a low carbohydrate diet while you are training, think twice if you do not want to feel awful a few days later. It's terribly difficult to function with low blood sugar.

(Note) Many amature bodybuilders, weekend warriors and inexperienced personal trainers will inform new comers to reduce carbohydrate intake to an unusually low level. DO NOT follow this advice. It's a dangerous, and irresponsible recommendation. "Low carb diet" may provide temporary results, but it's the long term results you should be striving for. "A sprinter can only go so far, but it is the marathon runner who goes the distance."

What to do in stage five?

- Allow yourself a cheat meal (two or three) times a week to combat the onset of the yoyo effect.
- Dropping carbohydrates at this stage to a low level is not recommended. Actually a very "low carb" diet taken on by individuals with little experience at this stage may serve as a trigger for failure. Inexperienced Comrades who test low carbohydrate diets have a high probability of experiencing low blood sugar and weakness.
- Making it to day 30 almost secures the foundation for long term success.

• Remind yourself why you are getting in shape. Have a poster or a picture in your car or room that reminds you every day to move forward.
• Go out and buy some jeans one size smaller and continue training to have them fit spot on.

• You made it to day 30, moving on to day 60 is just a blink away.
• Remind yourself that attitude is Key!

Step 6) Day 60 and onward!

To make it to day sixty says something about your character and the choice you made. It says that you have adapted to a difficult change, stayed organized and consistent. Something the majority fail to do. At this point you will have too much to lose if you stop. Turn day 60 into day 600 and you will be in the best shape of your life. 600 days is nothing in the grand scheme of things. When all is said and done, the time invested will go by fast, but the image you earn will be smiling back at you in every mirror. You will look back one day and remember the 60 days of fun. Then, you will look at the new and improved you 2.0 and continue on the journey. The first 60 days Comrade are the hardest for most ordinary people but not impossible. Make it to day 60 and do it right. Just don't lie to yourself. If you mess up, take responsibility and redirect the praiseworthy efforts back on track.

Factors that play a crucial role in success of achieving the Russian Ripped look

Self survey

Answer the following questions to yourself and rate the certainty of your answer on a scale of 1 to 10. One represents you disagree or the fact that you are not sure at all about the answer. Ten represents that you are truly sure of the answer and or you agree. If you answer any question with a certainty of less than seven ask yourself why that is and what you can do to influence a change in a positive direction. Do not lie to yourself and think about the answer. Take your time. This is for you and only for you so answer truthfully.

1) You keep a positive can do Comrade attitude when you commit to something.

1   2   3   4   5   6   7   8   9   10

2) You are an organized individual.

1   2   3   4   5   6   7   8   9   10

3) You do not allow random outside influences to interfere with your decision making.

1   2   3   4   5   6   7   8   9   10

4) You take responsibility for your actions.

1   2   3   4   5   6   7   8   9   10

5) You do not lie to yourself.

1   2   3   4   5   6   7   8   9   10

6) You believe in hard work.

1   2   3   4   5   6   7   8   9   10

7) You believe in yourself.

1   2   3   4   5   6   7   8   9   10

8) You always follow through on your plans.

1   2   3   4   5   6   7   8   9   10

9) You do not give up easily.

1   2   3   4   5   6   7   8   9   10

10) You understand that committing to a training program is not easy but you are ready, and you will, with all realistic effort, not give up because you want positive change.

1   2   3   4   5   6   7   8   9   10

Ok Comrade, now go back over all the answers and add them up. Do not read further if you have not added up the score.

If you scored a total of seventy points or more and answered truthfully you have a legitimate chance of making it past the first 60 days.
If you scored anything below seventy points, think why that is and what you can do about it to change the likely outcome. As silly as this all may sound, if you don't believe in yourself it will be almost impossible to continue with a strong and organized long term training program. The results are only as real as you are to yourself.

It's essential you understand and address the habits that can cripple you prior to starting any serious training program. You do not want to deceive yourself and waste time just to back track to day one over and over yo-yoing in the 60 day cycle. Many Comrades are in this yo-yo pattern because they do not address the harmful habits that are present outside of training.

1.   You keep a positive can do Comrade attitude when you commit to something.

If you do not remain positive, it will not be feasible to achieve the Russian Ripped look. You will run into situations where only your positive attitude can carry you through the rough spots.

2.   You are an organized individual.

Organization is a key factor that allows for a structured approach to training. Without organization the training structure is weak. "Not everyone is organized. But, organization is a skill that is attained through practice."
(Note) Start out by simply taking out a pen and a piece of paper. Then, start scheduling the tasks you need to do the following day every night before bed time. This easy writing exercise is a straightforward way to create a fast, yet sturdy foundation for organization. Taking it one day at a time is much better than going blindly through the typical daily motions.

3.   You do not allow random outside influences to interfere with your decision making.

Sometimes all of your friends want to party hardy Comrade. You can either go party with your friends and drink, or choose to go to bed early; so you can wake up early the following morning and train. If you are easily distracted and influenced it's an issue with priorities. You will need to ask the following question: Party like the rest or train to look your best? Choose wisely Comrade and keep in mind that parties and actions that lead to immediate gratification are always around. This is especially a challenge for the highly social butterflies who put a lively nightlife on a pedestal.

4. You take responsibility for your actions.

A Comrade who catches him or her self doing something that contradicts his or her goals is a Comrade who can recover. The recovery happens because the Comrade acknowledges the fact that he or she made a mistake and acts to reverse that mistake. To catch a mistake and not fix it is neglectful inaction. Neglect is a factor that will destroy any formal training program.

5. You do not lie to yourself.

Many decisions that we face must be evaluated first before taking action. A Comrade who does not fully analyze important situations and does not identify the reality based on a logical conclusion may take a wrong action. In a training program, wrong actions add up fast.

6. You believe in hard work.

Training is not easy. Some training approaches are established for the suitability of certain individuals. However, if you are a healthy Comrade, the way to a long term six pack is through hard work. This hard work is not a short term infomercial experiment. It's a long term commitment that requires long term dedication.

7. You believe in yourself.

Not to believe in one self is to relinquish opportunities and allow fears to influence decisions. When a Comrade fears something he or she may lack the follow through action on an important decision. Believe in yourself; get up every day and fight to win. "He who wants to win has passion to win. He who has passion has drive. Drive is the internal magic without which we can not significantly move forward."

8. You always follow through on your plans.

A big problem with some Comrades is the lack of persistence in stressful situations that block completion of set tasks. If you do not fall through on consistent training, it's a perfect set up for the yoyo trap. "This yoyo trap is like a rigged Tetris game. Half the time the blocks are rigged in your favor. The other half the time the blocks are purposely rigged against you."

9. You do not give up easily.

A tough Comrade has the edge. A tough Comrade already starts ahead of the rest and maintains the lead.

10. You understand that committing to a training program is not easy but you are ready, and you will with all realistic effort not give up because you want positive change.

This is self explanatory Comrade.

Please be true to yourself. Make the right decisions and move forward every day. To simply start training and not have fundamental questions answered that can clearly show you where you stand is not a good idea. Before you start a training program, understanding what your personalized priorities are is something you should not forget to visit. If a basic self checking evaluation process is left out prior to goal setting, the entire training approach automatically becomes a downgraded secondary priority that stands on a weak foundation. A secondary priority usually does not last because it lacks commitment and focus.

"Comrade Boris forgot to check himself and then he wrecked himself" Don't be like Boris!

Chapter 3 - Follow the Mirror Comrade, Not The Scale!

SELF MIRROR PICTURE FOR COMRADEBOOK

DAY 180

FOLLOW THE MIRROR NOT THE SCALE

DAY 1

Some Comrades do not necessarily agree with me on following the mirror philosophy. To some extent it's understandable, but let me tell you Comrade why I believe the mirror philosophy is king.

On the picture above there are two images. (Day 1 and day 180). The only thing I know about day one is that I was two hundred and forty pounds. That was one of few and perhaps the last times I was on the scale. What was my body fat on day 1? What were my measurements? I don't know Comrade and don't care.

Why?

Because I had the mirror philosophy to follow from the start and the mirror philosophy, works: It works if you decide to get in shape and not just create another weight loss resolution.

I said it before, and I will say it again. "Comrades are creatures of habit." One of the first habits that should be eliminated is the stepping on the scale to check the weight. This is an unhealthy habit that has psychological negative consequences attached to it.

When a Comrade steps on the scale and sees that no significant progress is made according to the scale, a mental trigger is activated that pushes the Comrade into a negative state of mind.

This trigger, activated by the scale number, applies to almost all Comrades who are fighting the good weight loss fight. The triggered negative state invites frustration and contributes to stress.

(Note) By going on the scale, in a moment the Comrade can fall from cloud nine and hit rock bottom. Stepping on the scale may also become an unwelcome chronic behavior of constant weight checking.
(Note) Checking up on the weight once a week is considered excessive.
(Note) If the Comrade consistently loses half or a quarter of a pound per week, he or she is doing great! Unfortunately, this low number is falsely considered to be insignificant and may not be noticed on the scale. I have seen a Comrade, we will call her "Comrade Masha" severely punish herself and regularly slip into unhappy moods; the scale was displaying numbers she did not like.

I asked Masha

"Why are you on the scale every day?"

She replied

"Because I want to track my progress."

I then asked Masha the following question.

"When you see a person, let's say you see a person in the gym. What is the first thought that runs through your mind?"

"I don't know," she replied.

"You mean you don't automatically ask yourself the question how much does that person you are looking at weigh?" Masha paused before she answered.

"Well if they are very out of shape I might think that, that person needs to get in shape or if the person is in shape I think wow! That person is looking good or -if the person is average looking I don't think anything." I shook my head and smiled.

"So actual weight number is of no importance to you, but the over all image might stir a thought, is that correct?" Masha nodded her head and said "yes, that's correct".

"So, if the over all image is the important thing, then why do you care about the scale so much?"

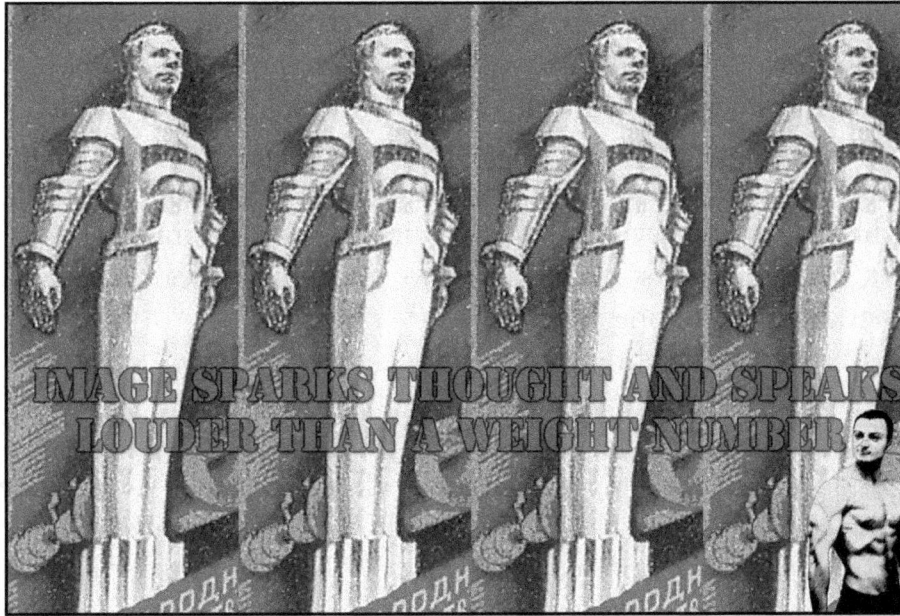

IMAGE SPARKS THOUGHT AND SPEAKS LOUDER THAN A WEIGHT NUMBER

Comrade Masha was focusing on the weight as the main and perhaps the only factor to gauge her progress. She became so obsessed with checking her weight she forgot to focus on the over all picture. The way to easily view the image progress is through the mirror, not the scale.

Now think about it Comrade. Do you truly care what someone else weighs? Or do you have a permanent mental representation of the over all image.

(Note) And yes Comrade, it's possible that as you train, body weight could fluxuate up and down as the waist line shrinks.

The scale can't tell you that the pants you now wear are fitting loosely. Maybe, after prolonged training you lose 20 pounds of fat, put on 8 pounds of muscle and retain 3 additional pounds of food and water. To the scale you only dropped 9 pounds, but according to the mirror the top two or four abdominals are showing.

Weight IS NOT a final determining progress factor! Remember that.

It is also a similar situation when it comes to measurements of separate body parts using some sort of tape measure. Not all Comrades are genetically created equal when it comes to muscle building and weight reduction. The physiques are all unique and different. The final results may not be what you like number wise on a tape measure, but in the mirror you can still see significant improvement. Some might have large arms, while others have small arms. Someone might have a genetically brawny chest while another person has tremendous calves. Everyone is different. Throw out the tape measure, you are not a measurement, you are not a number. You are an individual Comrade who can logically follow the whole body transformation process through the mirror.

For different reasons, Comrades follow different training philosophies when it comes to weight loss. But as a Russian Comrade who lives in the real world on a budget and understands the reality of what it takes, it's critical to be accurate without sugar coating anything. For example, when it comes to following the mirror: the type of training you do reflects truthfully and right back at you.

That means if you want to excel and see results every week while brushing your teeth, you have to set aside the mamsy-pamsy BS that's floating around on midnight infomercials, and if health permits, lift free weights, stick with cardio, the kind of cardio where you sweat and maintain a clean diet as a dominating food choice.

(Note) At twenty minutes a day three times a week the mirror will reflect a Comrade who is out of some money spent on some gadget.

The Russian Ripped look is something you must work for, but the pay off is remarkable. For a moment fast forward to twelve months from now. If you trained with commitment for twelve months and a person you have not seen for exactly that amount of time looks at you, it's almost a certain scenario that his or her jaw drops because you changed your image so much for the better.

Can you picture that moment twelve months from now?

The scale will never tell you what you look like. The first person to tell you that you are heading in the right direction is you looking back at you. So grab that camera or smart phone and take those progress photos of yourself every few weeks.

Now read on Comrade and focus on the overall big picture, not a number. And don't forget to smile.

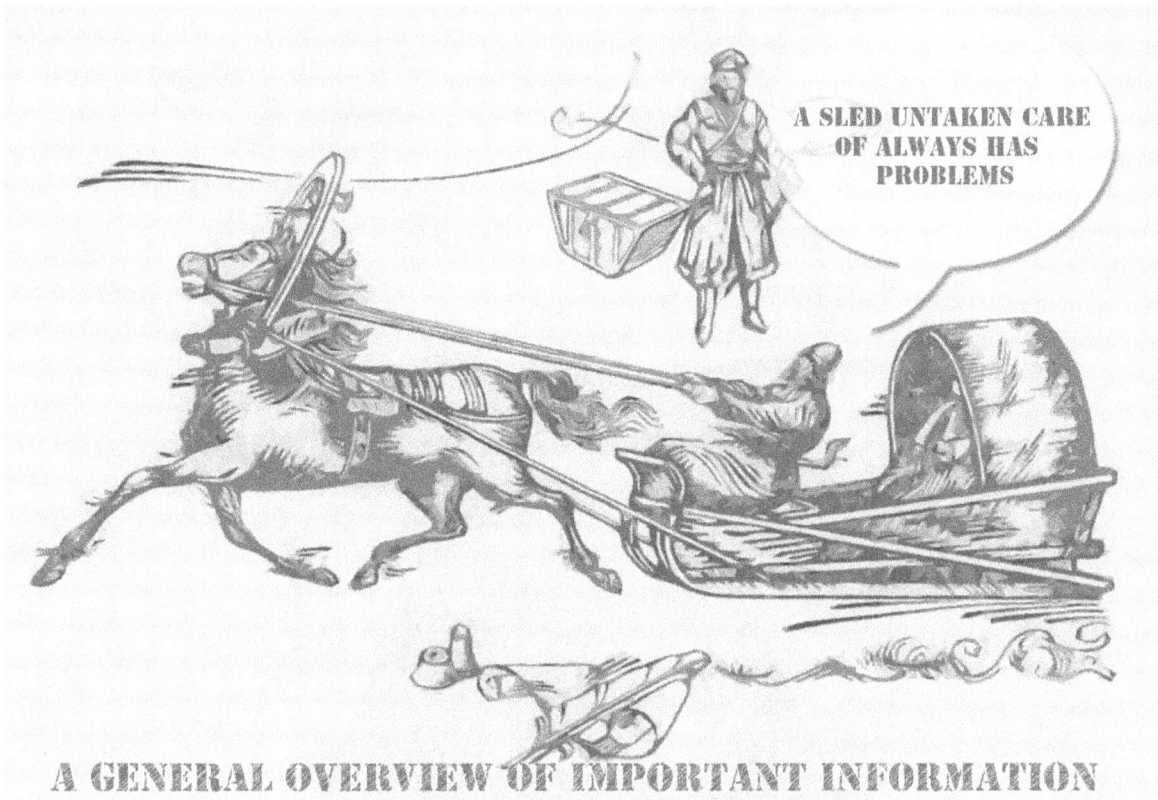

A SLED UNTAKEN CARE OF ALWAYS HAS PROBLEMS

A GENERAL OVERVIEW OF IMPORTANT INFORMATION

Chapter 4

I've been going to the gym and I'm still struggling to lose weight.

WHY?

This Chapter is a general overview for Comrades who wish to identify some of their potential past or present weight loss mistakes. The diagrams illustrate the difference between (weight loss) and (no weight loss or weight gain). Each general overview section is made up of two pyramid diagrams. The first pyramid of each section represents the Do's. The second Pyramid represents the Don'ts. If you fall into any of the Don'ts, that might be the reason for inconsistent or poor weight loss results.

The (Do's) Gym Training Pyramid. The first Do's pyramid represents a (90 minute in gym training session). The focus of this 90 minute training session is on weight loss.

The (Do's) Gym Training Pyramid

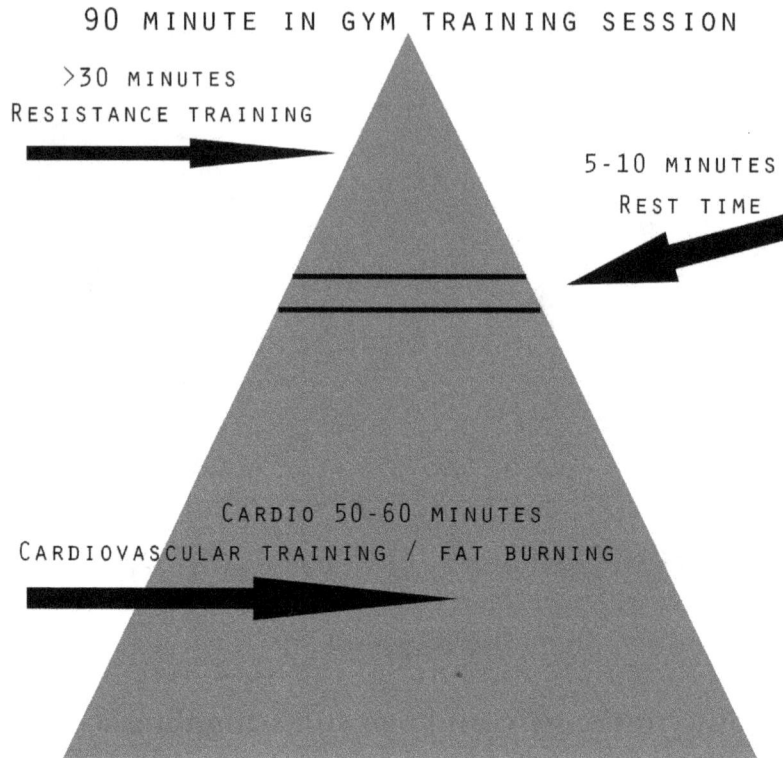

90 MINUTE IN GYM TRAINING SESSION

\>30 MINUTES
RESISTANCE TRAINING

5-10 MINUTES
REST TIME

CARDIO 50-60 MINUTES
CARDIOVASCULAR TRAINING / FAT BURNING

As you can see, the bulk of the training is directed towards cardiovascular / fat blasting training. This is the recommended approach towards (weight loss) when training in the gym.

The (Don'ts) Gym Training Pyramid

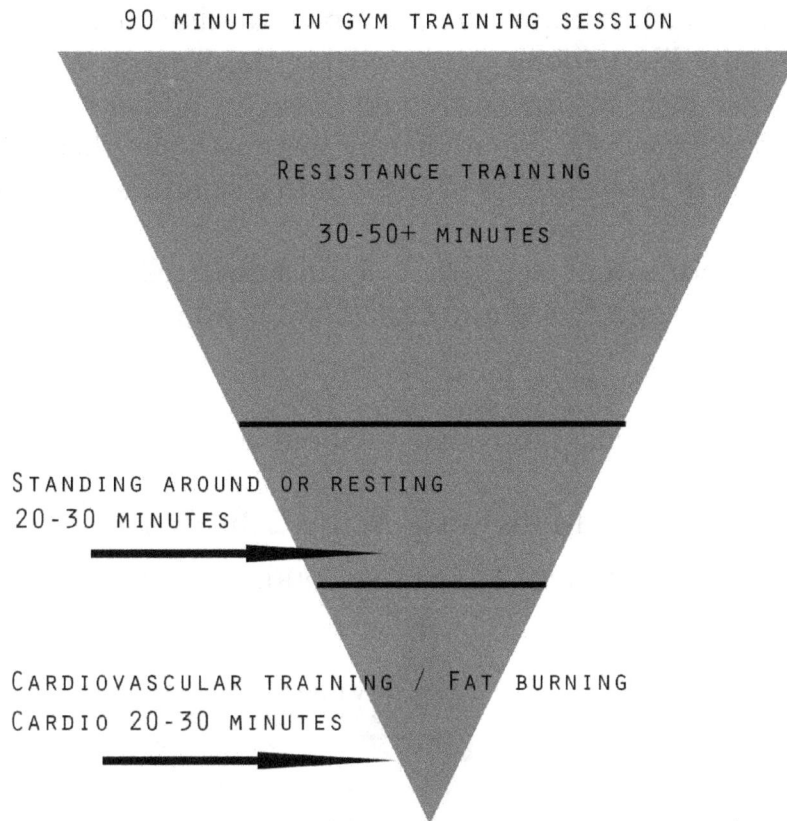

90 MINUTE IN GYM TRAINING SESSION

RESISTANCE TRAINING

30-50+ MINUTES

STANDING AROUND OR RESTING
20-30 MINUTES

CARDIOVASCULAR TRAINING / FAT BURNING
CARDIO 20-30 MINUTES

Overwhelmingly, the majority of Comrades who train in the gym take this approach. A Comrade might think that he or she is working towards a weight loss goal, but then why would weight lifting take precedence over cardio training? Why stand around for 20-30 minutes? Standing, sitting and waiting around usually occurs between workout sets. In weight loss, resistance training should not take priority over cardio/fat burning training. So, why then is this model typically followed by the majority?

A) Well, that's because this training model, unlike the Do's training model is easier to follow.

B) Because regular men mostly want to follow the macho, weight training method.

C) Because men who like the macho approach and know little about weight loss preach the macho approach to their friends, ladies, relatives and everyone else.

News flash!

60 minutes spent on the treadmill burns more calories than 60 minutes of classic resistance training, of which half the time is spent sitting around and recovering.
(Note) Some "fitness professionals" might disagree and say that resistance training is just as important as cardiovascular training. If the Comrade has more than 15lbs of fat to lose and does not plan on becoming a body builder, cardio/fat burning training takes priority.

The two following pyramid illustrations are examples of time management in a 24 hour period. The 24 hr pyramid illustrations are based on the Energy In Energy Out (EIEO) principle that follows basic daily mathematical caloric energy addition and expenditure. After examining both pyramids, you will be able to deduce that easy daily changes and incorporation of a proper 90 minute in gym training session adds up to a significant caloric expenditure over time.

(Note) I personally do not count calories. It's tiresome, tedious and time consuming. However, being aware of Energy In Energy Out (EIEO) principal is something that makes sense.

Example: A 500-600 calorie brownie can equate to about an hour spent on the Stairmaster, or 100 minutes on the treadmill.

The (Do's) Moderately Active 24hr Pyramid

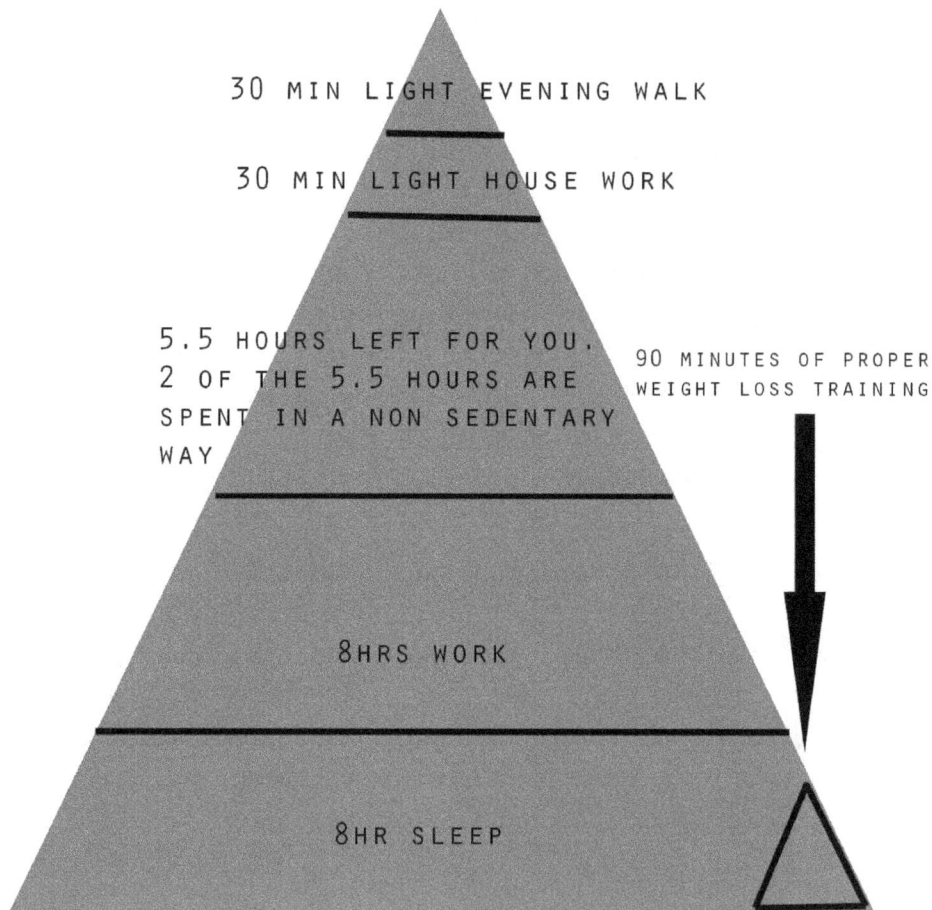

MODERATELY ACTIVE 24HR PYRAMID

30 MIN LIGHT EVENING WALK

30 MIN LIGHT HOUSE WORK

5.5 HOURS LEFT FOR YOU, 2 OF THE 5.5 HOURS ARE SPENT IN A NON SEDENTARY WAY

90 MINUTES OF PROPER WEIGHT LOSS TRAINING

8HRS WORK

8HR SLEEP

The (Don'ts) Standard Comrade 24hr Pyramid

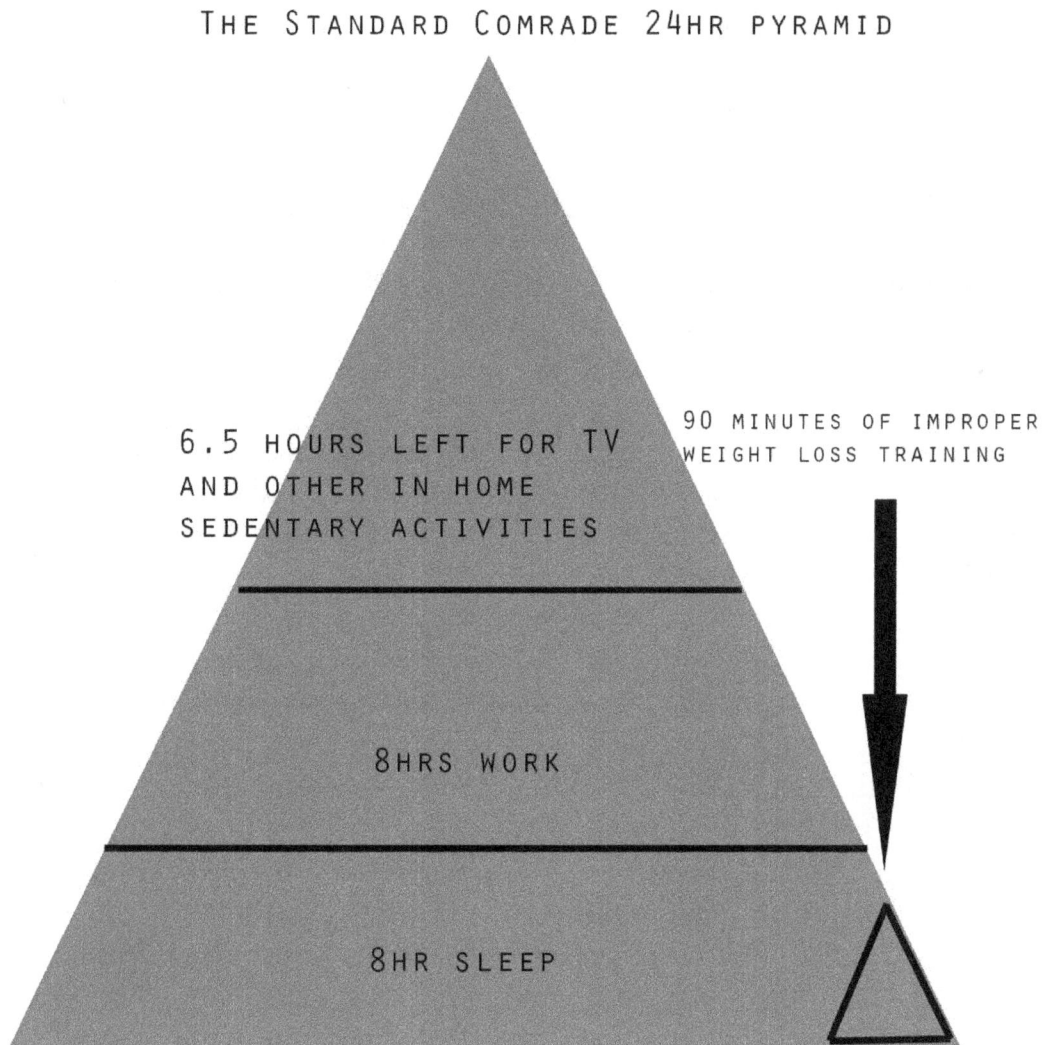

THE STANDARD COMRADE 24HR PYRAMID

6.5 HOURS LEFT FOR TV
AND OTHER IN HOME
SEDENTARY ACTIVITIES

90 MINUTES OF IMPROPER
WEIGHT LOSS TRAINING

8HRS WORK

8HR SLEEP

This pyramid illustration closely shows what the average Comrade might consider being a productive day (when referring to weight loss). The Comrade implements the improper 90 minute in gym training session and spends considerable amount of time in a sedentary state. What are the significant differences between the 24 hr (Do's and Don'ts) pyramids?

Standard Comrade 24hr pyramid
(Estimate) Improper 90 training = 300-350 negative calories for the day

Total (300-350 calories) burned

If a Comrade Consumed 2,500 calories that day, and burned off 300-350 calories, the total caloric consumption for the day is (2,200-2,150 calories).

Moderately Active 24hr pyramid

(Estimate) proper 90 training = (negative) 350-600 calories

(Estimate) 30 minutes light house work = (negative) 100 calories

(Estimate) 30 minutes light evening walk = (negative) 100-200 calories

Total (550-900 calories) burned

If a Comrade Consumed 2,500 calories that day, and burned off 550-900 calories, the total caloric consumption for the day is (1,950-1,600 calories). All though many other variables apply, at the lowest calculations, a 200 calorie difference is set between the two pyramids. **A pound of fat is 3,500 calories.**

That's a potential pound of fat lost every 17-18 days. (Other variables apply)
Yearly, that may come out to be 20-22 pounds lost or not gained. (Other variables apply)

(200 calories x 365 days = 73,000 calories / 3,500 calories = 20.56 pounds of fat)

The two following pyramid illustrations are examples of portion percentages of food consumed on a daily basis. All kidding aside this is relatively dry. None the less, the simplified information is valuable. "You are what you eat." With all respect to some fitness "professionals" and "dietitians" who never lifted a dumbbell or barbell in their life but possess the text book knowledge may disagree with the presented percentages. However, if the Comrade is in good health and is committed to drop fat weight, train hard and preserve lean muscle mass in the process, the pyramid percentages work as a general reference guide. More information regarding food is presented in the next chapter.

The (Do's) daily portion food percentages to reference

DAILY FOOD PORTION PERCENTAGES TO CONSIDER

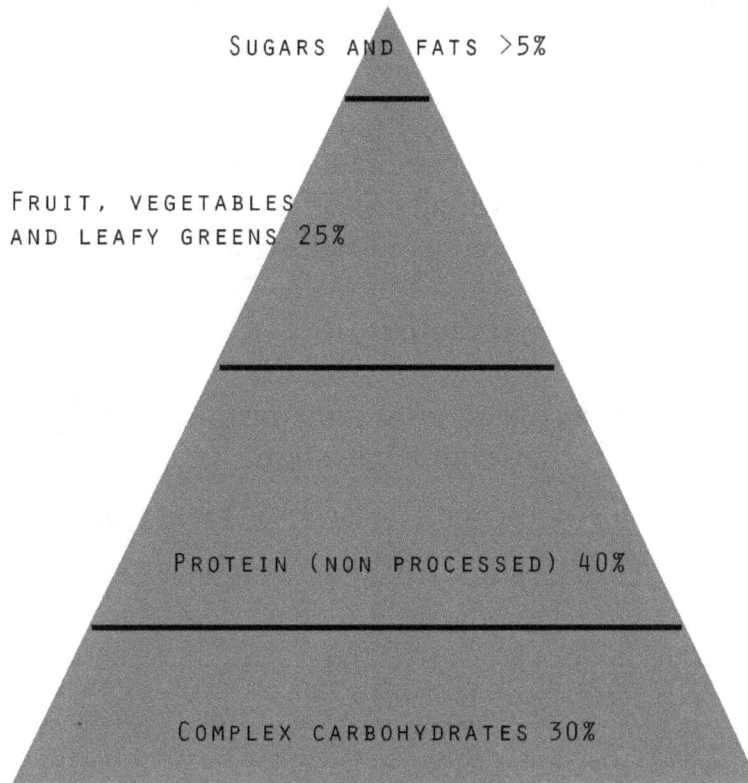

SUGARS AND FATS >5%

FRUIT, VEGETABLES
AND LEAFY GREENS 25%

PROTEIN (NON PROCESSED) 40%

COMPLEX CARBOHYDRATES 30%

The (Don'ts) common Comrade daily average food percentage portion ratio

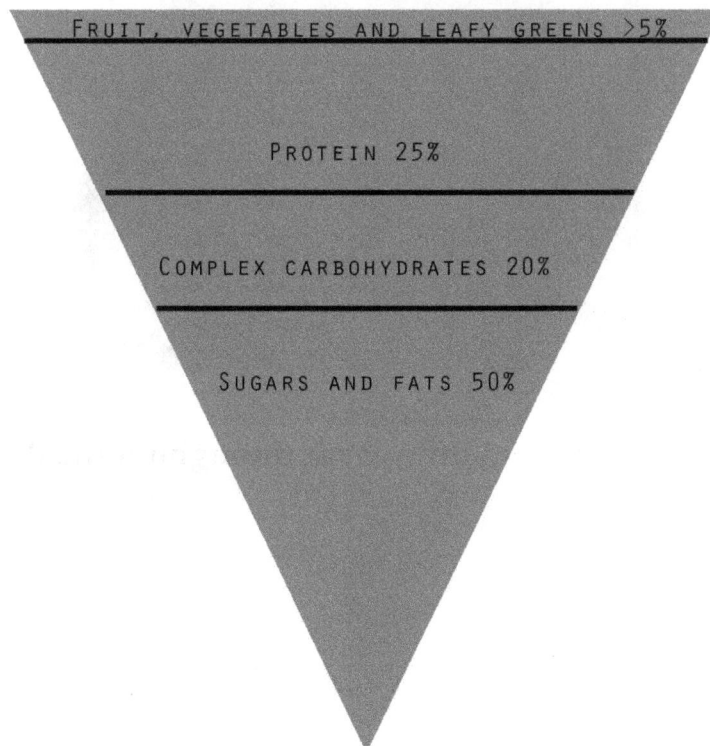

COMRADE DAILY AVERAGE FOOD PERCENTAGE PORTION RATIO

FRUIT, VEGETABLES AND LEAFY GREENS >5%

PROTEIN 25%

COMPLEX CARBOHYDRATES 20%

SUGARS AND FATS 50%

The (Don'ts) pyramid diagram is far from farfetched. It closely resembles an ugly truth. The truth is that numerous Comrades don't think about what they put in their bodies until health problems begin to scream at them. When those health problems happen, weight loss becomes a necessity, not a choice.

The two following pyramid illustrations are examples of eating consistency throughout the day. Some Comrades think that if they reduce the daily caloric intake, they will lose fat weight. This is not totally true. Lowering the over all caloric intake and allowing long periods of time to go by between meals will lead to lean tissue loss along with fat weight.

Lean tissue loss = slowing of the metabolism.

The (Do's) 2-3hr time gaps between food consumption for a positive functioning metabolic system.

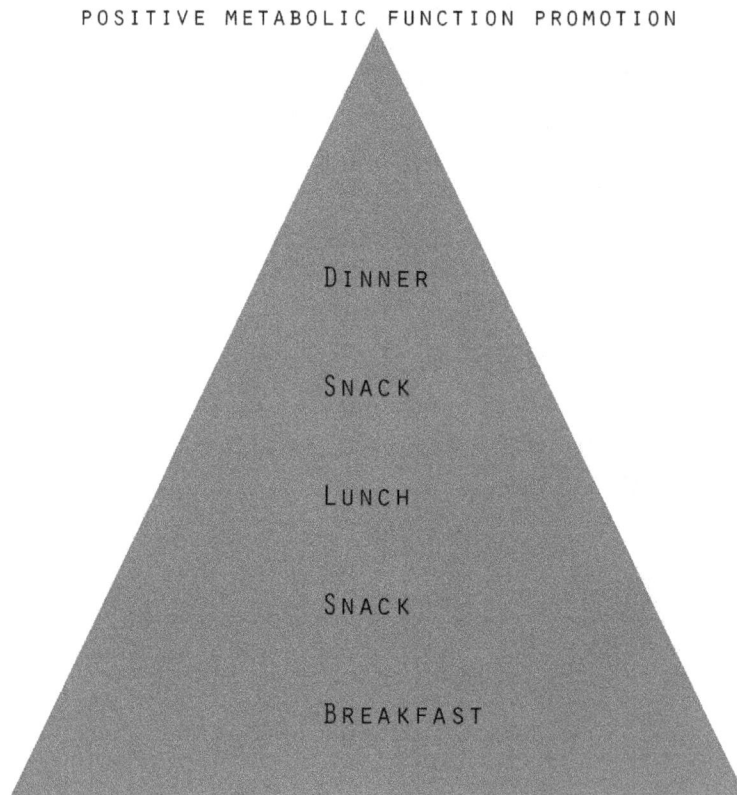

POSITIVE METABOLIC FUNCTION PROMOTION

DINNER

SNACK

LUNCH

SNACK

BREAKFAST

How many times do you eat throughout the day?

The (Don'ts) standard food consumption pattern

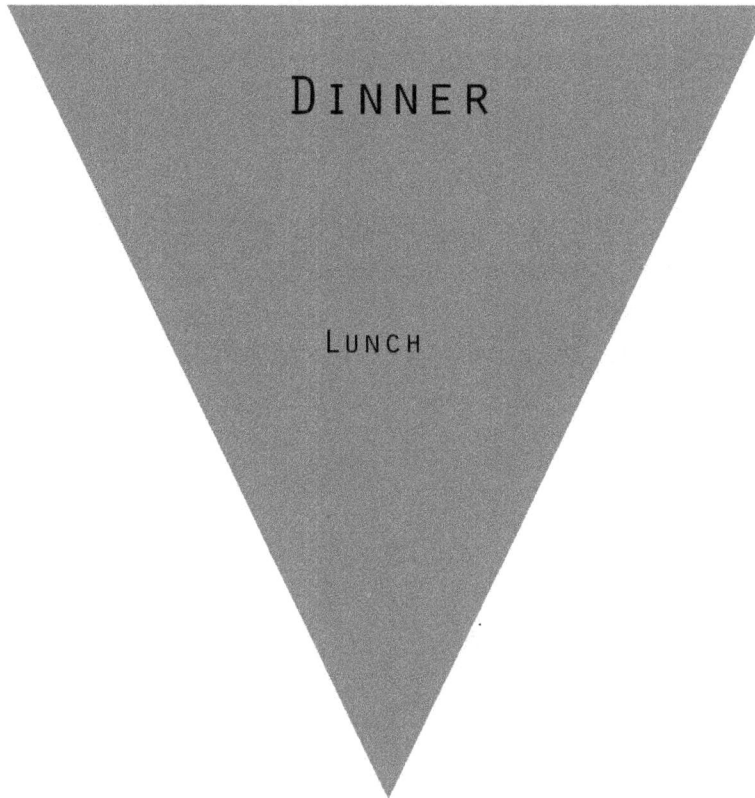

STANDARD FOOD CONSUMPTION PATTERN

DINNER

LUNCH

Skipping breakfast, having a normal sized lunch and a whopping dinner is a terrible choice for weight loss. This is actually the perfect storm for unhealthy weight gain. If a Comrade follows a diet that closely resembles the daily eating patterns from the Don'ts pyramid, he or she needs to rethink the current approach not to just weight loss, but health overall.

If we combine all the negative (Don'ts) triangles together, this is what we get:

1.   Improper training that does not optimize gym time to fight the fat.

2.   A sedentary lifestyle that does not burn enough calories consumed on a daily basis to maintain an equilibrium weight.

3.   High consumption of unhealthy fat and sugar calories.

4.   A slow metabolism because of unhealthy eating patterns.

If we combine all the (Do's) triangles together, this is what we get:

1.   Proper gym time utilization for optimal caloric expenditure.

2.   A lifestyle with some activity that requires additional calories to be burned through out the day.

3.   A balanced nutritional eating pattern that promotes the preservation of lean muscle mass.

4.   An efficient metabolism.

At times, we are not aware of what actions to take in order to fight the fat. If you are an avid gym patron who experiences weight loss problems, one or a combination of the pyramid illustrations may hold the answer as to why that is. Pretend that the each general overview section represents a tire on a car. Take away one tire and the car will not go very far.

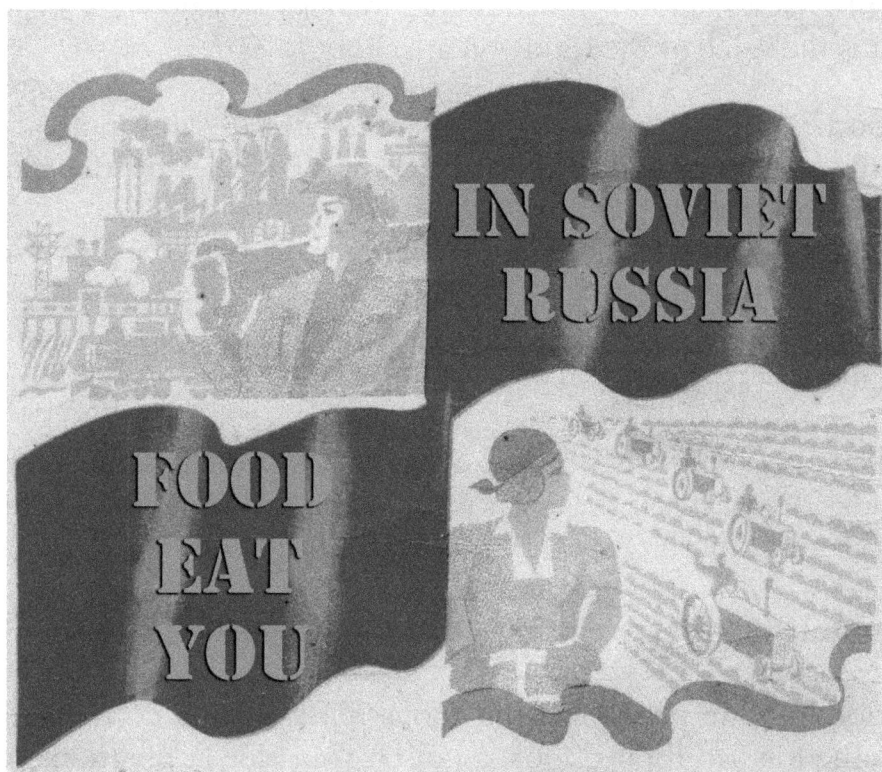

Chapter 5 - The Comrade Food

Food Comrade!
I try to keep it as uncomplicated as possible. I give you my word.

There's a terrific saying that I mentioned earlier. "You are what you eat." That saying is 100% accurate because no suitable image modification training program has ever succeeded without a good diet.

Now, unlike some other Comrades, I don't count calories. It's a terribly tedious and time consuming task to do. The calories do have significant value in weight loss, but it's the value of the food the Comrade puts inside his or her body that is of more importance than a caloric number.

I often hear that eating a low calorie diet regardless of what the food may be will help a Comrade loose fat weight. At first that may be so, but in the long run it's not worth it because the weight gain rebound and muscle loss are significant steps in the wrong direction. These backward steps have a tendency to accompany low calorie diets. Sticking to a low calorie diet with food that is of low value is like taking 3 steps forward and 4 steps back. To lose fat weight, prevent the loss of lean tissue, keep the metabolism running at optimum levels and avoid a weight gain rebound, the Comrade should eat frequent small portioned meals throughout the day. The food that's consumed in those small portioned meals must be of substantial value.

Eating 1000 calories of grilled salmon is not equal to eating 1000 calories of processed candy. The caloric value of grilled salmon is much higher than the caloric value of candy. Always ask the question, what is the value of the food you are about to eat?

Is it processed food? (Not a smart idea if you want to get Russian Ripped).
Is it high in sodium? (Not a bright idea if you want to elevate the blood pressure and possibly retain excessive water).
Is it high in fat? (Be kind to your arteries Comrade, if it looks greasy it's probably not healthy).
Is it high in sugar? (Control yourself). Don't eliminate sugar from the diet but do moderate the sugar consumption.

(Note) One of the worst things that can be done by a Comrade is the excessive drinking of the sugary soft drinks. It's like as if the sugar melts down and instantly contributes itself to the glorious @$$, sides and stomach. "Holy Borsh! Watch out Boris!"

Is the alcohol too much? (Empty calories in that shot Comrade, go easy).

It's not my intention to scare you, but if the above represent the dominating aspects of your personal diet then the Russian Ripped look is not on your side at the moment. Sorry if I snow on your parade Comrade. The good news is you can change that with basic knowledge. Just don't forget to act on that knowledge once you have it.

Carbohydrates- When you hear the word carbohydrates Comrade, think of fuel trucks. These trucks go inside your body and allow you to operate like a smooth mechanism. If you drop the fuel to exceedingly low levels, you will feel sluggish and out of energy. If you take in more fuel than necessary, the extra fuel gets set aside for a snowy day. For some strange reason Comrades all around the developed world believe that a frightfully distressing snowy day is always coming.
Some tasty carbohydrate sources include but are not limited to:
Oatmeal, buckwheat, whole wheat breads, potatoes and pasta.
1 gram of carbohydrates is equal to 4 calories

Protein- When you think of protein Comrade, think of engineers who come to build and repair different types of bridges and structures within the body.
Some quality protein sources include but are not limited to:
Chicken, turkey, fish, eggs and beef.
When the body is in a particularly unpleasant situation because it's been beaten up and not enough energy is available from carbohydrate sources, the engineers sacrifice themselves for the glory of your body. They are converted into energy. This happens predominantly to Comrades who go on a low or no carbohydrate diet.
(Not recommended)
1 gram of protein is equal to 4 calories

Fats

Saturated Fat- If it's a solid looking yellow lardy substance, most likely it's saturated fat. Prolonged high consumption of saturated fat elevates cholesterol levels and may lead to heart disease with other various health related problems.

Monounsaturated fats- These fats are present in but are not limited to: nuts and avocados. All Soviet peoples know that this type of fat helps with healthy cholesterol, and because of that, avocados are commonly consumed by the Russian Ripped Comrades.

Polyunsaturated fat- this type of fat is found in plants like corn and soybean. Small amounts may help reduce bad cholesterol, but too much of this type of fat may reduce the good cholesterol.

1 gram of fat is equal to 9 calories "Holy Borsh Boris! Yikes!"

Sugar- Go easy on the sugar and keep in mind that if you want to become Russian Ripped it's highly suggested you push the candy to the side. High sugar diets are remarkably unhealthy and contribute to obesity. Unfortunately, large percentage of Comrades living in developed society consume ridiculous amounts of sugar. In Soviet Russia we had a cure for obesity. It was called: "If you do less than 5 hours of cardio a day for 6 months you are handed over to the wild bears."

1 gram of sugar is 4 calories

Alcohol- put that Vodka down Comrade! 1 gram of alcohol is 7 calories.
Drinking a six pack of beer for example is 600 plus empty calories that promote a sate of dehydration. To burn off 600 calories the average Comrade must get his or her butt on the Stairmaster for over an hour. "Holy Borsh Boris! Yikes!"

Comrade hydration!

A Comrade in training must remember to stay hydrated. Water is the number one hydration option, and it should be consumed frequently through out the day. Fresh lemon juice mixed in together with water and ice also work. Iced tea is another excellent choice for hydration as long as it's not sweetened to the bone.
Sports drinks are a legitimate hydration option if you are truly sweating and training for tomorrow's war. However, many of the sports drinks are an overkill when it comes to the sugar content and unnatural chemicals.
(Note) In Soviet Russia we have a drink called Retoraid which contains 30 grams of sugar per bottle. That's like eating a trickers bar.

Water and iced tea always take the natural hydration lead. However, we are all human and sometimes a sweet liquid craving is necessary to satisfy. A good way to handle that is to make your own juice. Orange juice for example is by far one of the easiest juices to make. With the right equipment it takes less than 3 minutes. Sure orange juice is loaded with fructose (Fruit sugar), but it's natural, and you know what's in it because you made it.

Shopping Tips

• Stay predominantly on the outside ring of the supermarket.
• Shopping at the local 99 cent store is a glorious bargain Comrade. You can find frozen but clean meats, greens and a selection of low sodium seasonings.
• Check the back label of food packs. (4g sugar) Is about 1 tea spoon of sugar by volume. If you purchase a product that reads 12 grams of sugar per serving, that's about 3 tea spoons of sugar. "Holy Borsh!"
• Check the serving size! If a Comrade assumes the serving size without checking the back label, it doesn't necessarily make the guesstimate correct. The serving size of a product may be 2 or 3 times greater per can or bag than it seems. Eating the content of the whole bag or other product before checking the back labels may indicate the Comrade forgot to multiply the caloric, fat and sugar intake by 3 fold.
• If shopping for meat, pick out the leaner looking pieces, that way you don't over pay for the extra fat weight.
• If shopping for poultry, read the labels on the package. Some poultry is injected with salt and looks bigger and better at first glance. Often, no matter how long you clean and prepare this type of poultry, the salt taste will still be present even after it's cooked.
• Utilize the weekly coupons from local key supermarkets Comrade, I bought a pack of top quality sirloin steaks for $2.99 a lb recently. The regular price is $8.99 lb.
• A protein bar is not food! If you don't have the time to eat a full meal it doesn't mean you do not have 3 minutes to eat a small salad you should have prepared the night before. Also, see the back label of any protein bar you are interested in purchasing. Some protein bars taste delicious because they are loaded with sugar.
• Be sure to have enough water with you. The 16 oz grab bottles come in handy very often.
• Fish is not cheap, but fantastic deals are out there. Fish is by far one of the healthier ways to go. (Salmon, tilapia, cod, tuna, snapper).
• Whole wheat breads are a potent source of fiber and energy. The bread section is usually not located on the outside shopping aisles.
• Buckwheat is not sold in all stores; it's an excellent source of fiber and protein.
• Make a list before you go to the store and stick to it. "Deviation leads to fatty and sugary temptation."
• Use common sense Comrade. If you -for whatever reason must have some junk food do have some. Just don't make it a habit. "Just a little junk food every day keeps the abbs away but not the fat."

• Watch out for juices, many of them are just as worthless as sugary soft drinks. If you have the time and the ability, it's much better to make your own juices from fresh fruit or vegetables.

Simple food does the job

Before we get to some of the food preparation examples, I must mention that eating clean is not all that lavish if a Comrade is on a budget or doesn't have the time for proper meal preparation. The recipes about to be introduced are straightforward, and they work. Possibly you are far more creative than I, but unlike you, I had to live behind the iron curtain chasing bears in the snow all day long and fight random Spartans, wolves and other enemy infiltrators. I didn't have the time to fix grandioso banquets. Joking aside, the following examples will give you a solid start. I have 7 recipes to share with you that are as unpretentious as they come.

(Note) Monday through Sunday stay within the clean food eating plan, but on a Friday or Saturday night feel free to have a cheat meal. **A cheat meal is not to be confused with a cheat day.**

Comrade Greens

A tasty side dish that compliments meat dishes is known as the Comrade Greens. This side dish is remarkably easy to prepare, and it goes well with everything except the Yugo Fuel breakfast dish. I prefer to eat spinach as my first choice of Comrade Greens, however; broccoli, asparagus, and other green vegetables are a delightful addition to the mix. If you are one of those fancy shmancy Comrades, feel free to steam the greens and eat them hot.

For this side dish you will need:
1. Mixed greens of choice (I prefer spinach by itself)
2. Lemon
3. Deep bowl
4. Mixing spoon

1) GRAB A GOOD LEMON

2) CUT THE LEMON IN HALF

3) WASH THE CHOSEN GREENS

4) SQUEEZE HALF A LEMON INTO THE GREENS

5) MIX AND EAT

Tuna Salad

If a Comrade is on the go with little time to spare, the Tuna Salad option is a quick and clean one. The two variations of the dish are tuna from the can which is the cheaper option or if you have 5 extra minutes on hand with the extra cash, actual fresh tuna. In Soviet Russia all Comrades wait for a general store sale to stock up on fresh tuna.

For this dish you will need:

1.   Prepared Comrade Greens as a base.

2.   A grill (George Forman grill works perfect) if you are eating fresh tuna. Cooking time 3-7 minutes **(Note)** Soviet Russians love the Forman grill but the standard propane and charcoal grills are excellent choices too if cooking time is plentiful.

3.   If you are eating canned tuna, try to get the white albacore tuna in water.

4.   Mustard for canned tuna, low sodium seasoning of choice for fresh tuna.

Directions:

1)   Wash your hands.

2)   Prepare the Comrade Greens of choice for a base.

3)   Place grilled or canned tuna on top of the Comrade Greens.

4)   If the tuna is grilled, squeeze 1/2 lemon over the tuna.

5)   If the tuna is canned, add mustard on top.

6)   Congratulations, you may now eat, and you don't have to wait in line.

COMRADE GEENS

TUNA

GRILL

EAT COMRADE!

TUNA SALAD

The quick energy loading breakfast (aka) Yugo Fuel

As the Comrade wakes up, the whole day is ahead. This means that the Comrade is in need of energy. The morning time is where you fuel up your Yugo body (a remarkably dependable car) to kick start the day. Fueling up in the morning, instead of at night time, allows the body to burn off all or most of the fuel while functioning properly throughout the day.

(Note) Running on empty happens at times when Comrades skip the Yugo Fuel breakfast. Naturally the body hits the wall around lunch time. The typical reaction is to conceal this feeling with caffeine or a large lunch. This usually makes the situation worse.

(Note) The Yugo Fuel breakfast is particularly beneficial for the digestive system. It includes fiber and quality (Complex carbohydrates). It is not recommended to eat Yugo Fuel for dinner.

Yugo Fuel

For this dish you will need:

1) A selection of fruit: (banana, strawberries or blueberries). I like blueberries because they taste fabulous and there is no need to chop them up unless the Comrade lost his or her mind.

2) Plain (instant 1 minute) oatmeal, 1-2 cups. Simply eye the portion if no measuring cup is available.

3) About a tablespoon of honey

4) A small bowl

5) Water

6) Microwave that works

7) Tea spoon

Directions:

1) Wash your hands.

2) Pour 1-2 cups of dry oatmeal into the bowl.

3) Pour just enough water into the bowl to submerge the oatmeal.

(Do not drown the oatmeal in water)

4) Place the bowl inside the microwave for 1-2 minutes.

5) When ready, take the oatmeal out and place it on the counter.

(Handle the bowl with caution, it may be hot).

6) Move the oatmeal around with the tea spoon.

7) Throw fruit in the bowl.

8) Pour honey in a tic-tac-to pattern over the oatmeal and fruit.

9) Congratulations, you may now eat, and you don't have to wait in line.

BLUEBERRIES OR ANOTHER CHOICE OF FRUIT

PLAIN INSTANT OATMEAL

MICROWAVE

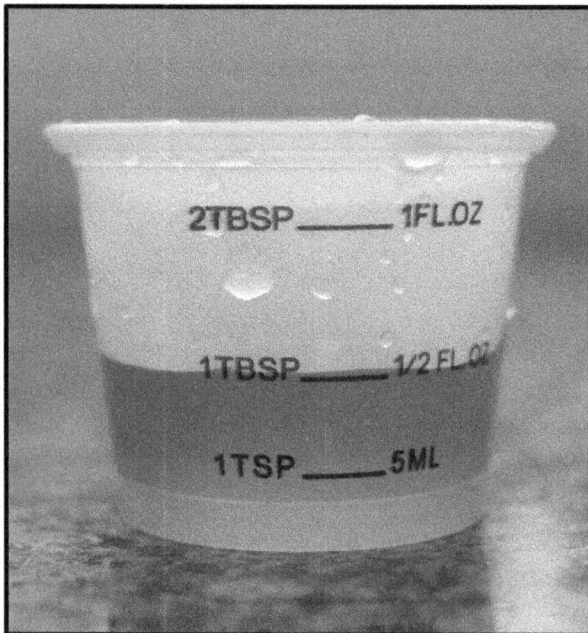

HONEY

WATER

SMALL–MEDIUM BOWL

TEA SPOON

EAT COMRADE!

YUGO FUEL

Tomato Ripped Omeletka

I know I know not everyone likes tomatoes Comrade. But here in Russia, where ketchup costs more than gold we replace it with tomatoes. If you don't like tomatoes just leave them out. As for me, the tomato goes in as well as onion, mushrooms and cilantro. This omelet is rich in protein, and low in fuel (complex carbohydrates). The Omletka is an excellent dinner choice. It's common that this dish is enjoyed by itself without a side. However, if a Comrade is very hungry a slice of toasted Russian Black bread adds a crunch. (The traditional supermarkets do not sell Russian black bread Comrade, sorry).

For this dish you will need:

1. Frying pan

2. Toaster (optional)

3. Cooking spray

4. Egg whites (supermarkets sell plain egg whites in milk carton packaging; they should be conveniently located by the butter).

5. Chopped tomatoes (optional)

6. Chopped onions (optional)

7. Chopped cilantro (optional)

8. Mushrooms (optional)

9. Slice of black bread (optional)

10. ½ Avocado (optional) but recommended

11. Pepper or low sodium seasoning

12. Mixing spoon

Directions:

1) Wash your hands.

2) Spray the pan with coking spray.

3) Place the pan on a low fire.

4) Throw in the chopped tomatoes, onions and mushrooms. (Optional)

5) Stir the tomatoes and onions until the onion starts to change color and the tomato skin starts pealing.

6) Pour about a third of the small sized egg white package content into the pan. Roughly 5-10 oz. Depending how hungry you are determines the pour. Just don't overdo it.

7) Slowly stir.

8) Sprinkle cilantro and add a low sodium seasoning. (Optional)

9) Continue stirring until the egg whites harden and everything inside the pan is thoroughly mixed.

10) Carefully place the omelet on a plate.

11) Congratulations, you may now eat, and you don't have to wait in line.

OPTIONAL SIDES

CILANTRO

BLACK BREAD

TOMATOE

ONION

AVOCADO

LOW SODIUM SEASONING

MUSHROOMS

FRYING PAN

TOASTER

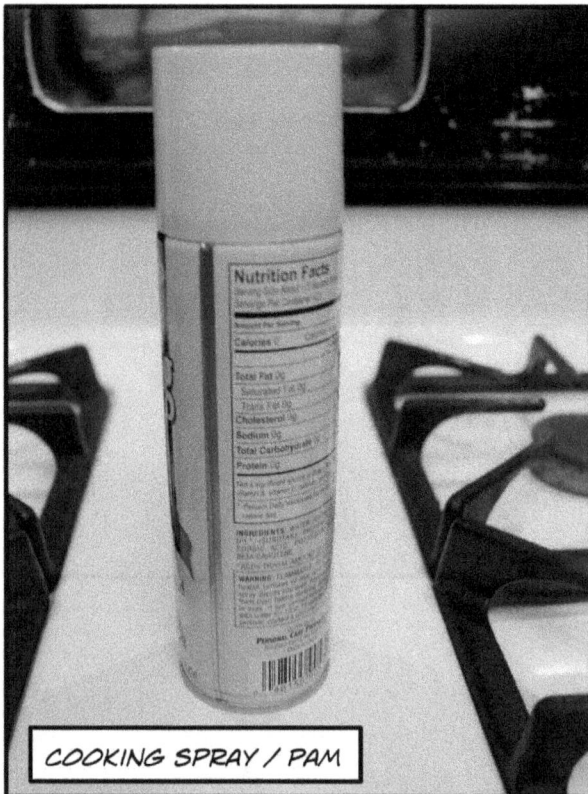

COOKING SPRAY / PAM

EGG WHITES

EAT COMRADE!

TOMATOE RIPPED OMLETKA

Standard Comrade Meal No.1

The Standard Comrade Meal No.1 is a very standard high protein meal designed to build the Comrade strength. It's by far the most standard, affordable and popular meal that is consumed by the top secret Russian Ripped generals to stay in glorious shape.

For this dish you will need:

1. A grill (George Forman grill works perfect) or a standard grill

2. Electric steam cooker

3. Cutting desk

4. Sharp knife

5. Chicken breast

6. Buckwheat

7. Low sodium seasoning of choice (I prefer dry garlic)

Directions:

1. Wash your hands.

2. Place 1-2 cups of buckwheat into the steam pot.

3. Rinse the buckwheat out at least two times.

4. Fill the pot with twice the amount of water in relationship to buckwheat.

5. Close the steam pot and remember to turn it on. Wait 10-15 minutes before moving on to the chicken.

6. Place a skinless chicken breast on the cutting board and cut off the fat if any is present.

7. Cut several strips side by side half way through the chicken breast.

8. Sprinkle a low sodium seasoning on the chicken breast.

9. Remove the chicken from the cutting board and place it on the grill.

10. Close the grill lid and turn the grill on.

11. Wash the cutting board thoroughly.

12. After about 10-15 minutes on the grill, the chicken should be cooked. A crispy outer layer will begin form on the chicken breast.

13. Congratulations, you may now eat, and you don't have to wait in line.

GRILL

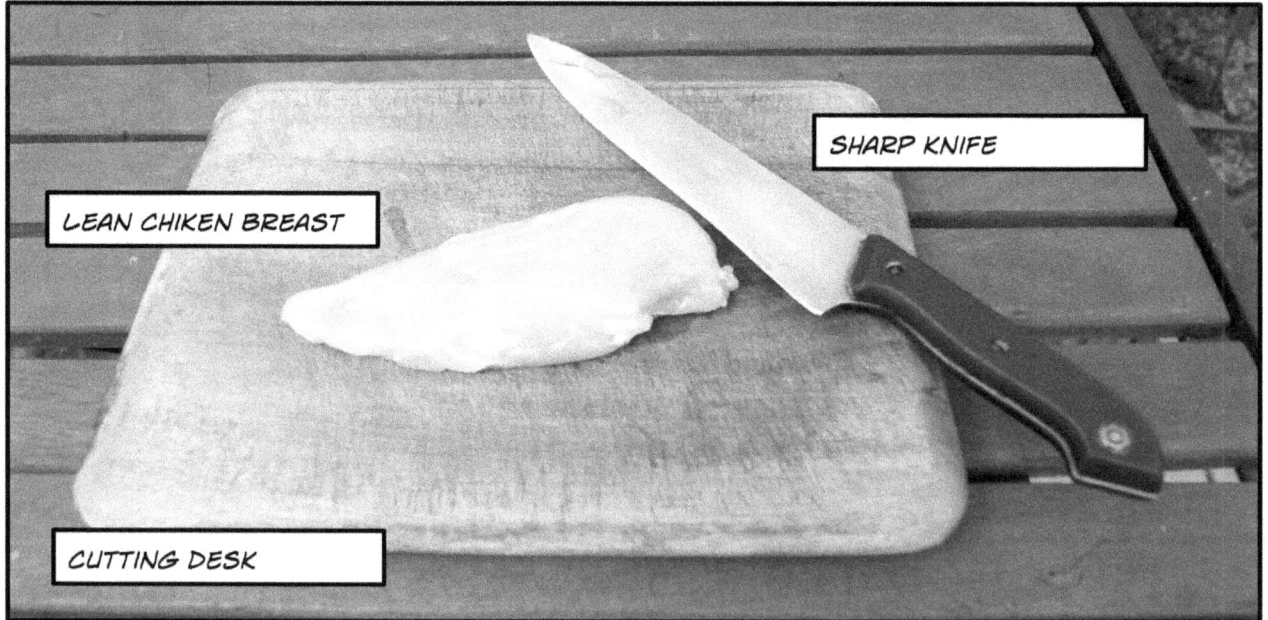

SHARP KNIFE

LEAN CHIKEN BREAST

CUTTING DESK

ELECTRIC STEAM COOKER

BUCKWHEAT

Ilya Sulima

EAT COMRADE!

STANDARD COMRADE MEAL NO.1

60

Standard Comrade Meal No.2

The Standard Comrade Meal No.2 is by far one of the most favorite meals of the Russian Ripped Generals. They like it because it's easy on the digestive system and it tastes better than chicken. If any Comrade has the opportunity to eat this meal at least once a day, it will significantly benefit him or her in the grand scheme of abdominal showing power.

For this dish you will need:

1. A grill (George Forman grill works perfect) or a standard grill

2. Electric steam cooker

3. Cutting desk

4. Sharp knife

5.   Clean Fish filet (I like salmon the most but tuna and tilapia are also healthy choices. If you prepare tuna, don't keep it on the grill to long because it dries out quickly.

6.   Brown rice

7.   Comrade Greens (optional)

8.   Asparagus (optional).

9.   Seasoning of choice (I prefer any low sodium seasoning).

Directions:
1.   Wash your hands.

2.   Place 1-2 cups of brown rice into the steam pot.

3.   Rinse the brown rice out two times.

4.   Fill the pot with twice the amount of water in relationship to brown rice.

5.   Close the steam pot and remember to turn it on. Wait 10-15 minutes before moving on to cook the fish.

6.   Place the fish on the cutting board and cut a piece you would like. (Go easy Comrade and cut a small or a moderate piece).

7.   Sprinkle a low sodium seasoning on the fish.

8.   Remove the fish from the cutting board and place it on the grill.

9.   Close the grill lid and turn the grill on.

10. Wash the cutting board thoroughly.

11. After about 5-10 minutes the fish should be ready to eat. First few times you make this dish be sure to check on the grill often not to overcook the fish.

12. If you wish to add other sides like the Comrade Greens or asparagus feel free to do so.

13. After you remove the fish from the grill, placed it on a plate and squeeze lemon all over the fish without mercy. Congratulations, you may now eat, and you don't have to wait in line.

GRILL

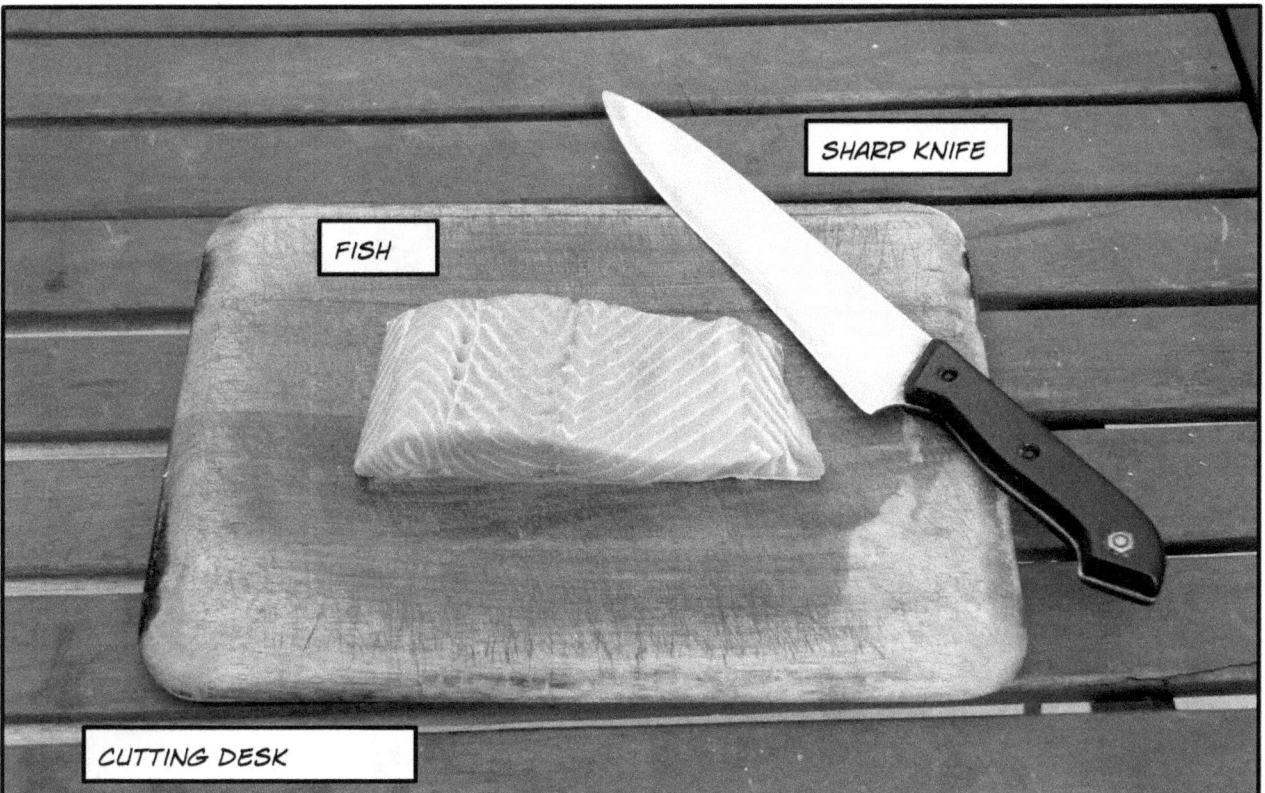

SHARP KNIFE

FISH

CUTTING DESK

ASPARAGUS AND
LEMON (OPTIONAL)

ELECTRIC STEAM
COOKER

BROWN RICE

EAT COMRADE!

STANDARD COMRADE MEAL NO.2

Standard Comrade Meal No.3

The Standard Comrade Meal No.3 is a meal that is very much liked by the Russian Ripped Generals. However, this meal is not recommended to be enjoyed more than once or twice a week. This meal puts the digestive system into overdrive. None the less, it's a glorious meal that helps with maximum Comrade power and muscle development.

For this dish you will need:

1. A grill (George Forman grill works perfect) or a standard grill

2. Working microwave

3. Cutting desk

4. Sharp knife

5. Potato

6. Clean piece of meat

7. Seasoning of choice (I prefer any low sodium seasoning or dry garlic for this dish)

Directions:

1. Wash your hands.

2. Place the meat on the cutting board and cut a portion you would like. (Go easy Comrade and cut a moderate piece).

3. Sprinkle a low sodium seasoning on the meat.

4. Remove the meat from the cutting board and place it on to the grill.

5. Close the grill lid and turn the grill on.

6. Wash a medium size potato.

7. Poke some holes in the potato with a knife and place it into the microwave for 5-6 minutes.

8. Wash the cutting board thoroughly.

9. After about 6-12 minutes the meat should be ready; depending on how you like it cooked.

10. Remove the steak from the grill and place it on a plate.

11. Remove the potato from the microwave and place it on the plate.

12. Congratulations, you may now eat, and you don't have to wait in line.

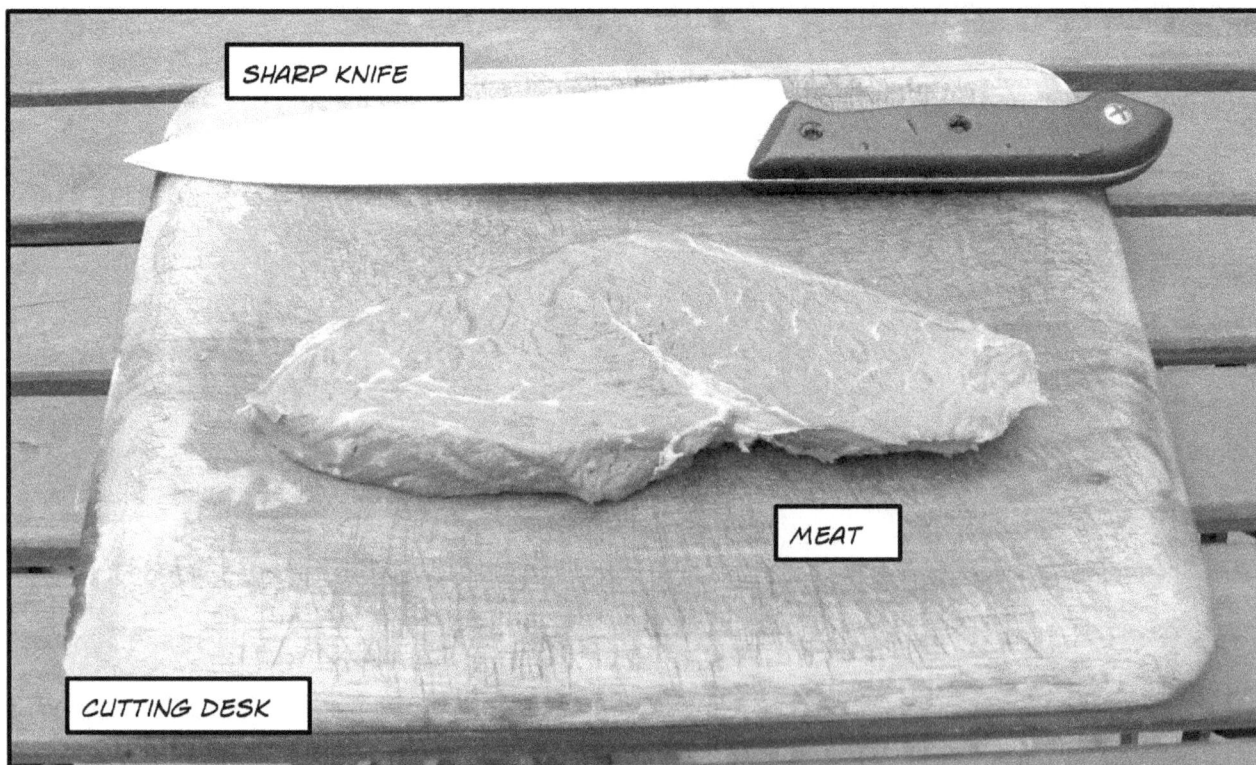

MICROWAVE

POTATOE

EAT COMRADE!

STANDARD COMRADE MEAL NO.3

Fruit- Natural Energy Snacks

Adding fruit to the diet is a convenient way to increase natural vitamin intake and satisfy a sweet craving. It's recommended eating fruit regularly throughout the day. Many Comrades choose to eat apples, bananas, strawberries, oranges, grapes and blueberries immediately after workouts to replenish the lost energy with natural sugar from fruit.

(Note) Some Comrades have a terribly distressing gas reaction when mixing bananas with protein shakes. So be kind and don't release poisonous gas for the public to enjoy.

Additional General Food Information

If the Comrade is healthy, without any specific dietary prescriptions, the basic examples below show estimated (general time schedule guidelines) for when a Comrade should eat depending on the daily workout schedule.

Approximate scheduled training time 7:00am-9:00 am

6 am) Yugo Fuel

7-9 am) Training time

9:30 am)-(Orange Juice + BCAA's (Branch Chain Amino Acids) Standard Comrade Meal # 1 or a (protein shake if the Comrade has no time to eat)

Lunch) Standard Comrade Meal #1 or the Tuna Salad

5 pm) Standard Comrade Meal #2

Dinner) Tomato Ripped Omeletka

Approximate scheduled training time 12:00pm-2:00 pm

6 am) Yugo Fuel

11am) Tuna Salad

12-2 pm) Training time

2:30 pm)-(Orange Juice + BCAA's (Branch Chain Amino Acids) +Standard Comrade Meal # 1 or a (protein shake if the Comrade has no time to eat)

5:30 pm) Standard Comrade Meal #2 or (#3 a maximum of 2 times a week)

Dinner) Tomato Ripped Omeletka

Approximate scheduled training time 6:00pm-9:00 pm

6 am) Yugo Fuel

10 am) Standard Comrade Meal #2 or (#3 a maximum of 2 times a week)

2 pm) Standard Comrade Meal #1

5 pm) Tuna salad

6-9 pm) Training time

9:30pm) Orange Juice + BCAA's (Branch Chain Amino Acids) + Tomato Ripped Omeletka

----

Side notes – A

• It's a good idea to power up for breakfast. (Yugo Fuel) First meal of the day should have the most complex carbohydrates unlike other meals.

• The post workout meal should include some form of recovery aid like (BCAA). More information on supplementation is covered in the next chapter.

• The last meal of the day should have little or no carbohydrates. (Omletka)

• The Standard Comrade Meal #3 is heavy on the digestive system and should not be consumed frequently throughout the week.

• Protein shakes are a last line of defense. If a Comrade is interested in growing muscle, it's common practice to consume a few protein shakes throughout the day.

Side notes – B

1. If no post workout recovery drinks or BCAA's are available, a standard protein drink does a terrific job as a post workout replacement.

2. If choosing between a terribly unhealthy meal and a protein shake, go with the shake to reduce significant amounts out unhealthy calories.

The Comrade Pravda Word

Ok Comrade. As far as food goes, you now have a convenient starting point towards the Russian Ripped look without the rocket science attached to it. No need to get scientifically fancy. Just stick to the basics.

1. Be prepared for the following day. Lack of organization will jeopardize your Russian Ripped goals.

2. Drink plenty of water. Yes you will probably visit the bathroom more often.

3. Eat every few hours. Eating often through out the day will speed up the internal engine (metabolism). Eating jumbo meals once or twice a day like many Comrades do is a very, very, very poor choice. Try to avoid eating big meals as if a bear is chasing you and you are not letting go of the honey that the bear wants. Let the honey go! Eat small and eat frequent.

4.   Fuel up in the morning. Do not skip breakfast.

Comrades have a tendency to over think food and diet. Do not complicate it so much but feel free to slowly introduce more food variation by mixing up some sides. Einstein said it best. He said "If you do the same thing over and over and expect different results you are crazy." Well, Mr. Einstein I have to correct you on the topic of food and getting in shape. If you train over and over and eat clean over and over you will achieve phenomenal results. Just be patient and consistent.

This chapter is a basic and straightforward guide for you to reference. But by all means continue learning about food and nutrition if you want to understand the rocket science behind the rockets. As a great general once said to me "You can lead a bear to vodka, but you can't make him drink it. Vodka is vodka, it's simple, and it always does the trick. I don't know why some bears get fancy and try to mix and add other things to this pure product that works. Simplicity, that's the key."

Stay strong, keep it simple in the food department and get Russian Ripped.

Chapter 6 - General Comrade Supplements

Notice: Consult with a physician before taking any kind of supplementation. Most dietary supplement statements on the market today have not been evaluated by the FDA.

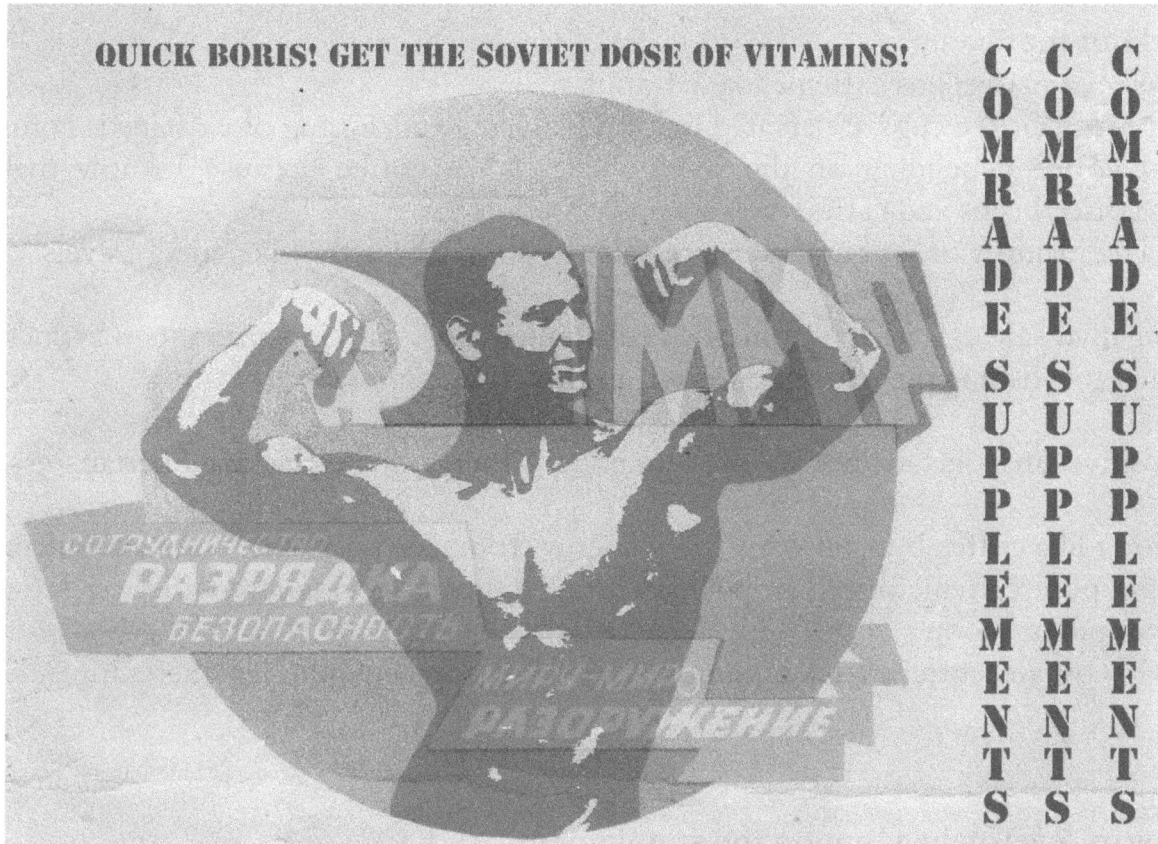

Please Comrade always remember rule # 1
(Do not supplement food with supplements)

I have seen countless numbers of Comrades spend ridiculous amounts of money on chemicals. Then many of them complained because no significant results were made. I'm not saying that all supplements are harmful. On the contrary, Comrade, some supplements are like fast rollerblades. If a hungry bear decides to chase you down a paved hill, the rollerblades help you cover more distance in a shorter period of time. With a clean diet and a solid exercise program supplements help a Comrade achieve certain set fitness goals faster. However, workout supplements taken alone (not in combination with physical training and a clean diet) will not get the Comrade very far.

(**Note**) If you take the time to do independent research on supplements, you will find out that many supplement companies lack scientific studies to support their claims. For some companies it's just a matter of sugar, caffeine and fancy packaging. To be Russian Ripped doesn't mean to just be ripped. It means to also be healthy like a track horse. Eating large quantities of chemicals vs. eating nutritious food of value may have adverse effects in the long run.

So, now that we got that part out of the way lets move on to some information about basic rollerblades that may make you faster and perhaps (help or hurt) you get away from the bear.

Pre workout motivator

Coffee, what a marvellous caffeine loaded drink.

(Note) Not all coffee cups are created equal. On average 60-120mg of caffeine is contained in a cup of coffee depending on the serving size. I like coffee because I know that coffee contains coffee beans and caffeine.

(Note) The majority of fat burners use caffeine as a main base to spike energy levels.

Some negative side effects for Comrades consuming large caffeine amounts may include but not limited to: Visiting the bathroom often, anxiety, restlessness.

Some positives may include but are not limited to: Energy, focus, kicking Spartan @ss.

If you don't like coffee but still want some energy from clean caffeine, you have the option of purchasing pure caffeine in pill or powder form. Average serving strength ranges from 100-200mg per pill or scoop.

(Note) If you are currently taking any pre workout supplements, are there any side effects like:

Crashing
Low energy levels when, not on the supplement
Sleeping problems
Becoming easily irritated
Visiting the restroom frequently
Dry mouth

If any of the listed symptoms above happen, it may be related to the amounts of pre workout supplementation consumed. It's not recommended to take stimulants for long periods of time since the body builds tolerance and thus always requires larger amounts to maintain same energy feel.

(Note) If the Comrade becomes addicted to a fat burner or energy supplement and decides to stop. After a hard energy crash he or she will probably have an unpleasant low energy week.

Home Made Orange Juice

Home made orange juice may serve you as a potent natural energy supplement. How?
Orange juice is loaded with sugar, natural sugar aka fructose. When OJ is combined with BCAA (Branch Chain Amino Acids) it works as a reliable delivery system for BCAA.

(Note) Think of sugar as a school bus, the BCAA as the students, and the final destination as the school or the muscles. The students get to school faster when they take the bus instead of walking all the way.

(Note) Post workout drinks usually have some kind of bus system with BCAA and other ingredients.

What is needed to make orange juice?

1)   3-4 oranges

2)   An apparatus that squeezes oranges (electric preferred)

3)   A clean glass with your name on it

If you take a trip to the 99 cent store, you have a high probability of finding a cheap but effective plastic orange squeezer. 1) Cut the orange in half. 2) Rotate the orange with some pressure around the round form. Usually it takes 2-5 minutes to make juice this way.

If you have some extra cash to spend I would highly recommend an electric orange juice machine. It takes about 30 seconds to finish off 3 oranges.

Branch Chain Amino Acids (BCAA)
Branch Chain Amino acids can be thought of as engineers that the body doesn't manufacture but recruits from food. The body calls out for BCAA exceedingly often to make mandatory repairs. BCAA, like protein powders, help with various body care functions; one of those functions is aiding in muscle repair.

Protein powders
Protein powders like (BCAA) help Comrades recover after exercise, and they also aid in muscle growth. Usually protein powders are consumed in large amounts by bodybuilders, power lifters and other serious athletes. Protein powders are not a bad idea if you are trying to put on some lean weight. However, protein powders can also help reduce caloric intake while promoting the preservation of lean muscle mass. Protein powder is the next best thing to food in a pinch when the Comrade needs to eat but unquestionably has no opportunity to do so.

(Note) Drinking a protein shake right after a workout is common practice.
(Note) A down side to drinking protein is the fact that if a Comrade is hungry, it will not always leave him or her in a state of pleasant satiety after consumption.
(Note) Prolonged hunger has a tendency to influence mood. To combat this, food must take precedence over protein shakes. Always!

Glutamine

Glutamine is an amino acid that favors muscle recovery. It's said that glutamine reduces soreness and helps improve protein utilization. If a Comrade was training very hard he or she will experience muscle soreness. Glutamine would be a glorious recovery aid to utilize for that type of situation.

(Note) Glutamine is often prescribed to burn victims to aid in the recovery process.

Creatine

Let me tell you a secret about some nifty rollerblades Comrade. This secret is called creatine. To keep it simple, creatine deals with cell energy. "It promotes additional bear like strength and pushing power around the gym."

(Note) Always read the supplement back label for directions. Many times the recommended serving size is 2-5g per serving.
(Note) Creatine is primarily for Comrades who want to gain strength and put on some muscle.
(Note) Most of the time a Comrade who uses standard creatine can expect some water retention.

Fish oil* (Yes please)!

In Soviet Russia all Comrades who lack fish in their diet always take fish oil softgel caps with their meals 2-3 times a day. Fish oil helps fight the fat and supports the heart. "Russian Ripped Comrades take fish oil daily as if the glory of the motherland depended on it."

(Note) Fish oil is generally taken with meals.

Multi Vitamins

If a Comrade has been eating a poor diet for a long time with limited amount of fruit, it's a good chance that he or she is in need of a multi vitamin.

(Note) Not all vitamins are created equal. If the back label reads something like 1000% of the daily value for any ingredient, common sense should tell you that it's an overkill to use that particular vitamin type. (Unless your doctor specifically said you need to).

(Note) If you are already taking some other pre or post workout supplements remember to check if any vitamins and minerals are a part of those supplements. If you don't check the back labels and take multi vitamins with other supplements in combination, it's possible that you are getting a 10,000% daily dose of some particular vitamin or mineral as a result.

Check the back labels!

Liver care

The liver is the power house that must be taken care of Comrade. It's the nutrition logistics center of the body. If the liver goes, any Comrade on the receiving end is in a world trouble. I highly suggest taking an interest in liver care products especially for Comrades who have prolonged experience with alcohol, energy drinks or consumed large quantities of fatty junk food in the recent years.

(Note) It's a good idea to do yearly blood work just to be sure everything is working the way it should be Comrade.
(Note) If the Comrade thinks that his or her liver is in trouble, the Comrade should see a doctor immediately before taking any kind of dietary supplementation.

Joint Care

Like multi vitamins, numerous supplement companies are promoting joint care products. There are plenty of options to choose from. A Comrade should look for products containing Glucosamine and Chondroitin.

(Note) Ask your doctor if you need to take this stuff. Some Comrades have banged up connective tissues so for them joint care is important. For other Comrades who have no problems in this department should take care of their joints by not doing anything stupid like lifting extremely heavy weight.

Fat Burners and Energy Drinks

Common sense Comrades! Do you have it?

First of all this stuff may be unsuitable for your stomach, thyroid, and liver. Educated Comrades who take fat burners have specific extreme goals in mind. These Comrades are body builders getting ready for competitions. These are fighters cutting extra weight before a fight. These are movie stars getting ready for a specific fit role.

(Note) Fat burners are extreme fat loss aids for extreme goals. Fat burners are not necessary in the long run if you follow a clean diet.
(Note) Comrades taking fat burners for a long time will build up a tolerance towards them. Larger quantities become necessary to feel the same stimulation jolt.
(Note) Any Comrade who takes fat burners must always stay hydrated!

Bottom Line on Supplements

Ok Comrade, thousands of companies are out there selling all sorts of supplements. Some of these supplements might be made in China or in someone's home with low grade products. I'm not implying that all supplements are harmful, but none the less it's better to always be careful about the things you put in your body. Have you ever tried reading the back label of some supplement products? I have. It was like having a drunken Russian speaking bear that doesn't speak English read the ingredients in English and translate out loud back to Russian. "Holy Borsh! Confusing!"

(Note) reading blog posts and reviews on the internet about the product that interests you is something you might always want to do.

(Note) If you have health problems, get them taken care of through a doctor before buying a bunch of pills or powders that could potentially augment your health.

(Note) Would you buy a $1,000 dollar car for $50,000 dollars? That's how it is with some supplements. In some cases you are overpaying for glorified sugar.

(Note) Look for products that are (GMP) –Good Manufacturing Compliant and are manufactured in an FDA approved facility. It should be written on the package.

(Note) Something new in the supplement industry comes out every five minutes.

(Note) If a Comrade walks into a supplement store he or she might get lucky and learn something about supplementation from an exceptionally knowledgeable professional. However, at times that is not the case. Sometimes it's just a teenage kid behind the counter with little experience.

A bear walks into an (RNC) Russian Nutrition Corner and say
"I want something to lose weight."
The rabbit salesman looks at the bear and says
"Here take this, it works for the wolf."
The bear say
"I no wolf I bear."
Rabbit salesman says
"If it works for wolf it works for bear."
Bear say
"How you know this?"
Rabbit salesman says
"Because it says so on the can, see, it says ultimate weight loss formula."
Bear say
"Well if it's written on the can, if it looks flashy and you are exited about it how can it not be true?" Rabbit say
"Exactly, that will be $45.99."

Bear bought the product and left. Little did bear know that he bought a product that was full of caffeine combined with a diuretic.

(Note) The bear will eliminate some water weight and feel a jolt from the caffeine thinking the product is working. The actual retail value of that product was $3.99.

Gym Etiquette

Because no one wants to hear a loud
"OMG, Like, Whatever"
phone conversation.

In Soviet Russia, the gym is the church.
Disrespectful behavior is punished by 8 hours of
consecutive cardio. And someone always stands
behind you with a loaded gun yelling "faster! faster!
You stop, you die!"

Chapter 7- Gym Etiquette and other Important Considerations

The gym is a place where exercise equipment is conveniently placed for Comrades who want to become Russian Ripped. It makes logical sense to train in a gym. In Soviet Russia, I remember bench pressing rocks in the forest. It wasn't fun because the rocks were always of different weight and grabbing them was a pain in the @$$. So, if you have the option to use the gym, please use that option.

(Note) Because so many Comrades have not the slightest indication of unspoken gym rules, I will list some of them and also include general pet peeves, gripes and rants. (Enjoy)

1) The gym is not a place for a Comrade to loudly talk on the phone. It's annoying and rude. It becomes twice as annoying if the Comrade is talking on the phone and sitting on a piece of equipment that someone else might want to use.

2) Filling up a bottle with water at the drinking fountain when someone is waiting behind you is exceptionally rude. Most likely the person behind you just wants a quick two second drink. Let that person or people go ahead of you and then proceed to fill the water bottle. It's like as if five motorist want to make a right turn on a street at five am but can't because one

slow pedestrian is taking his sweet time crossing the street pissing everyone off and blocking traffic from moving on.

3)   Placing the weights back in order shows that the Comrade actually cares and has respect for others.
(Note) It's tremendously frustrating to look for a 25lb dumbbell on the other side of the gym where it doesn't belong.

4)   Unless the Comrade is in phenomenal shape, it's against Soviet Russian law to wear a tight shirt or a wife beater. If the Comrade is in shape, he or she earned the right to wear a tight shirt.

5)   For Comrades who wear glasses; (Never put them on the floor for any reason). I had heard on two occasions the crunching sound of glasses when they were accidentally stepped on. Then I heard something like "What the hell did you do to my glasses bro?" (That's the clean version).

6)   If you are the type of Comrade who follows the bodybuilding philosophy please, for the love of everything that is holy don't forget to train your legs! It's funny to see Comrades with stunning upper bodies and stick figured legs. And don't blame it on genetics.

7)   Do not use a ridiculous amount of weight that's more than you can properly handle. Proper technique with light to moderate weight is safer and does a Comrade more over all good. It's hilariously entertaining to see someone squat heavy weight and only go down 6-12 inches. No need to show off Comrade, just do the exercises properly.
(Note) As funny as it may be to watch a Comrade use heavy weight and do the exercise wrong, it's a particularly dangerous situation that could end up terribly bad.

8)   Watch out for salesman personal trainers prowling like wolves on the gym floor. Many trainers know what they are doing when it comes to training others. However, in the fitness industry a large percentage of trainers are known as paper trainers. What is a paper trainer? A personal trainer with a paper that says he or she is certified to train but lacks actual experience. If you are interested in personal training always ask for the trainer's: credentials, experience and a minimum of five references (and then call them all).
(Note) Does the trainer look the part too or does he or she just sound smart?

9)   If you are in shape Comrade, showing off in front of the mirror is exceedingly egotistical unless you are training in a hard core gym where bodybuilding and power lifting philosophy rules. Modesty is always a smart thing. This somewhat contradicts the fourth point made earlier. Regardless, modesty shows maturity and no one likes a douchebag.

10) Unless you; are a cyclist, have back problems, just starting to exercise or have other medical issues, the stationary bike is not for you. Get your butt on the treadmill or the Stairmaster and sweat! No pain, no gain.

11) Be aware of the surroundings, the gym is full of metal. Fatigue and rigorous training may cause a Comrade temporary disorientation. Walking into metal is no fun. I am guilty of this.

12) Texting on the treadmill is a striking example of an accident waiting to happen.

13) Call 911 if a Comrade is using dumbbells at the same time he or she is on the treadmill or Stairmaster. Ok don't call 911 but tell the gym personnel immediately. It's not safe.

14) Do not leave empty drink cans on the gym floor.

15) Ladies please, when working out, do not wear high heel shoes, boots or anything that elevates your height and shifts pressure towards the toes. This goes for lady personal trainers as well. It's an accident waiting to happen. Use common sense please.

16) Wipe down equipment after use. Because no one wants to put their head in the sweat puddle you left behind.

17) Sometimes a music listening device helps greatly if you train without a workout partner. On my music device I have the Soviet Anthem on a loop, and it's the only song I ever listen to.

18) If you know what you are doing before you enter the gym, training time will progress in a productive manner. **(Note)** No grownup wants to look like a lost child in the grocery store. Plan ahead.

19) "I want to workout, but I don't want to get bulky." I heard this saying a million times. Comrades, please, for the love of everything that is holy unless you are training heavy and hard you will not get muscle bulky. My dear lovely ladies, if you ever say these words to a personal trainer that's the first give away sign you are an easy sale and know very little or nothing about working out. Instead of saying "I want to workout, but I don't want to get bulky." Please say something like "I'm interested in learning about how to (Fill in the blank), what are your recommendations?"

20) To all the teenagers and other common sense lacking Comrades. No one wants to hear you blast your own personal music on speaker mode through a smart phone or another device. The gym is not a personal night club. Have respect for others and use headphones.

21) Ladies please relax on the perfume.

22) Don't be a part of a gym Cluster F*** Group. What is a Cluster F*** group? It's a bunch of obnoxious individuals who are loud and/or act stupid in the gym. In Soviet Russia we have no tolerance for offensive idiots in the gym.

23) Be polite.

24) Show respect

25) If sweat isn't on your body shortly after you started to exercise, you are not training hard enough.

LENIN BUILD!
LENIN PARTY!
LENIN RIPPED!

17) SOMETIMES A MUSIC LISTENING DEVICE HELPS GREATLY IF YOU TRAIN WITHOUT A PARTNER. ON MY MUSIC DEVICE I HAVE THE SOVIET ANTHEM ON A LOOP AND IT'S THE ONLY SONG I EVER LISTEN TO WHEN WORKING OUT.

Comrade Gear

Weight lifting gloves- Not all gloves are created equal. Some gloves have wrist support while others do not. If a Comrade is training in the gym, the gloves help prevent calluses.
(Note) Ladies please safeguard your lovely hands and wear gloves if training with free weights. Just a suggestion.
If the Comrade is training outside the gym, gloves may serve as protection and comfort.
(Note) Gloves especially help with pushups; when they are performed outside on rough or cold terrain.

Shoes- If the Comrade is training legs in the gym or swinging a heavy kettlebell, he or she should be wearing a shoe with a flat sole. If the Comrade is running on hilly terrain, a hiking hybrid running shoe will do the job. For other basic running needs a standard running shoe should be worn. In Soviet Russia a man wearing slippers once tried to get away from a bear. He did not get away because the bear was wearing running shoes.

Clothing- Yes Comrade, black shirts make a Comrade look slimmer and white shirts make a Comrade look bigger. If the Comrade wants attention, he or she should wear bright yellow. But seriously Comrade, if it's hot, wear shorts, and if it's cold, put on some sweats. If you are out of shape, cover up and don't wear tight clothing. In Soviet Russia it's not permitted to wear a wife beater shirt unless the Comrade is in incredible shape.

Weightlifting belt- Comrades that stick close to the bodybuilding and power lifting philosophy usually use belts on exercises that involve heavy lifting. It's a terrific idea to use a belt if a Comrade is about to squat or dead lift heavy weight.

Wrist straps- Some Comrades use wrist straps to help them do more: pullups, shrugs and deadlifts. Some say wrist straps are only used by weak Comrades who have puny grip power. However, if a Comrade trains with very heavy weights, they may be difficult to hold on to without wrist straps. "I don't care how many times you squeeze that hand grip squeezer thing to strengthen grip power. Shrugging a 200lb dumbbell in each hand will still require wrist straps."

Knee wraps- Like wrist straps, knee wraps serve a purpose when training legs with heavy weight. Knee wraps are not a fashion statement so don't get exited Comrade.

Digital camera- This is a powerful handy device to have on hand for progress pictures. Challenge yourself to take a full body Myspace style picture every few weeks to keep track of progress. In Soviet Russia Myspace is called Ourspace so that all comments may be shared equally amongst the Comrades and bears. If a Comrade is taking a progress picture every month and no change happens between the pictures, then he or she should logically conclude that diet or training needs improvement.

(Note) If you use a smart phone to take progress pictures, don't accidentally share the pictures on a social network without thinking twice.

(Note) A self full body shot is not to be taken from above in an "Emo, look at me way." Please take the pictures head on.

Hygiene- Many times I have experienced other Comrade smells that were offensive and borderline illegal. Please shower. Unlike in Soviet Russia, you always have hot water. Use it!

Lifting journal- If you are not a powerlifter or a bodybuilder and you simply need to lose weight, a lifting journal is not necessary. In the long run, it doesn't matter if you lift some weight 16 or 17 times.

(Note) In the gym the Comrade must sweat, not write a life story on how many times he or she curled a barbell.

Chapter 8-Basic in Gym Stretches and Training Philosophies

The Russian Ripped training method is a combination of several training philosophies. Bodybuilding, powerlifting, circuit training and unorthodox military training are all a part of this approach. Having multiple choices at hand, no Comrade is required to integrate all philosophies to achieve the final ripped look. For gym dwellers, following the basics and progressing through those basics is more than enough to get the job done.

If a Comrade wishes to train more like a mixed martial arts fighter, a particular training option is available for doing so outside the gym.

For Comrades who are easily bored, multiple philosophies may be tied in together to change things up.

Stretching and Warming up

Not even Russians like to get injured Comrade so certain steps are taken to ensure for a lesser chance of injury.

"One day bear woke up in the middle of winter and decided to go outside to bench press some tree trunks. Afterwards, long hours of excruciating pain and discomfort stayed with him for weeks, reminding him to always warm up and stretch before doing any physical training."

(Note) Think of the warm-up as a force field that protects you from ravenous wolves. Now pretend that these wolves are always out to get you in the first few minutes of training. To strengthen the force field you should follow some of the following recommendations listed below prior to actual training.

First

Assess what the temperature like? If it's cold, be sure to cover up and keep warm. When the temperature is cold, the Comrade increases the chances of pulling or tearing a muscle. If the Comrade trains in a warm environment, the chances for muscle injury decrease.

Second

If the training is to take place in the gym, start off with a ten minute warm up (treadmill) session to break a sweat. If the training is outside the gym, a slow 10 minute jogging session should get the blood, oxygen and the joints moving. Do not skip this step.

Third

Identify the specific training to be done for the day. If training in a gym environment, usually certain body parts are chosen and thus stretching those body parts after a quick cardio warm up is a good idea. (Some may argue that stretching before lifting weights saps some strength away from certain lifts). To which I say "It's better to be safe than sorry so stretch." If the training for the day is performed outside the gym, it's a good idea to perform multiple stretches. Whenever a Comrade trains outside, he or she should stretch a few minutes longer. (See examples of the Comrade select standard stretches)

Comrade select standard stretches:

THE STANDARD QUADRICEP STRETCH

TOVARISH! DON'T FORGET THE STANDARD QUAD STRETCH. JUST BECAUSE IT'S STANDARD DOES NOT MAKE IT LESS IMPORTANT.

GENERAL QUADRICEP STRETCH

TO PERFORM THIS STRETCH, THE COMRADE NEEDS TO STAND AND BALANCE ON ONE LEG WHILE HOLDING THE ANKLE OF THE OTHER LEG. IF THE COMRADE CAN'T MAINTAIN BALANCE, HOLDING ON TO SOMETHING IS RECOMMENDED AS WELL AS LOOKING AT A FIXED POINT IN THE FRONT. HOLD THE STRETCH FOR ROUGHLY 20-30 SECONDS ON EACH SIDE.

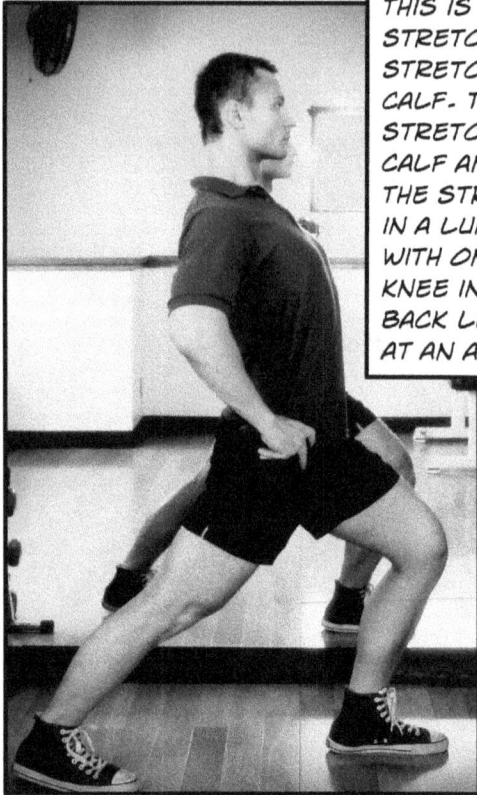

THIS IS A TWO PART STRETCH. THE FIRST PART STRETCHES THE BACK-LEG-CALF. THE SECOND PART STRETCHES THE BACK-LEG-CALF AND THE HIP FLEXOR. THE STRETCH IS PERFORMED IN A LUNGE LIKE POSITION WITH ONE LEG BENT AT THE KNEE IN THE FRONT AND THE BACK LEG KEPT LOCKED OUT AT AN ANGLE.

THIS IS A PARTY APPROVED STRETCH

CALF AND HIP FLEXOR STRETCH

THE SECOND PART STRETCHES THE BACK CALF AND THE HIP FLEXOR. FOR A LIGHT STRETCH, LIFT THE SAME SIDE ARM AS THE FRONT LEG. IF YOU WANT A DEEP STRETCH, LIFT THE ARM OPPOSITE SIDE OF THE LEG IN FRONT AND LEAN BACK.
HOLD EACH PART OF THE STRETCH FOR ROUGHLY 20 SECONDS ON EACH SIDE.

GLORIOUSLY PLACE ONE LEG OVER THE OTHER AND APPLY PRESSURE TO THE KNEE WITH YOUR HANDS.
HOLD THIS STRETCH FOR 20 SECONDS TWO TIMES ON EACH SIDE.

TO ALL MY RUNNER COMRADES. THIS STRETCH ESPECIALLY CONCERNS YOU. I MEAN, WHAT IF A BEAR POPS OUT FROM SOMEWHERE AND STARTS TO CHASE YOU? IF YOU DIDN'T STRETCH, YOU COULD PULL SOMETHING AND END UP AS LUNCH!

THE STANDARD INNER THIGH AND HIP STRETCH

STANDARD HAMSTRING STRETCH

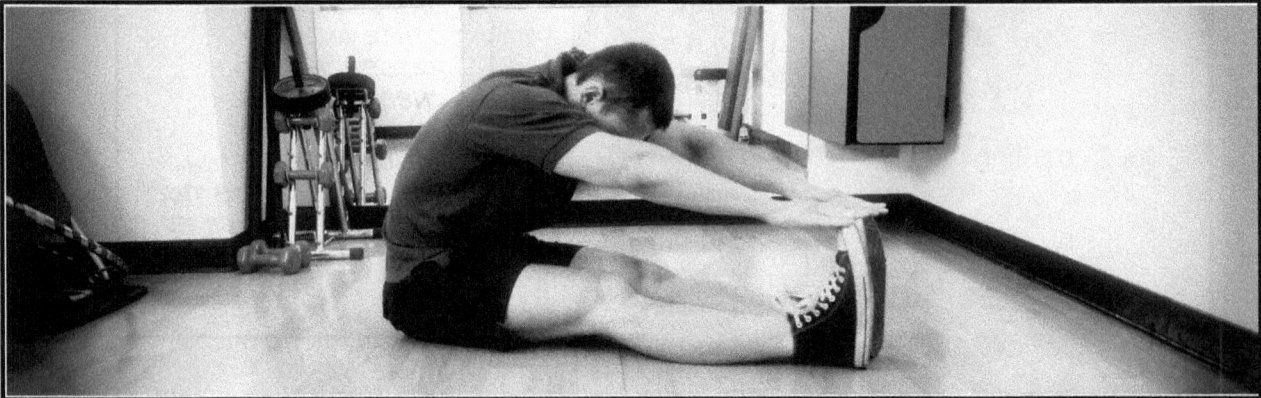

THIS STRETCH IS PERFORMED ON EVEN GROUND. WHILE SITTING DOWN THE COMRADE SHOULD TRY TO REACH FORWARD WITH THE FINGERS AS FAR AS POSSIBLE TOWARDS THE TOES AND HOLD THE STRETCH AT THE FARTHEST POINT OF TOLERABLE DISCOMFORT. THE STRETCH SHOULD BE HELD FOR ROUGHLY 20-30 SECONDS TWO OR THREE TIMES.

STANDARD ABDOMINAL STRETCH

STRETCH THOSE ABBS COMRADE! LIE DOWN ON THE GROUND, LIFT THE UPPER BODY UP WITH YOUR ARMS AND HOLD. ALONG WITH THE ABDOMINAL STRETCH, YOU WILL FEEL MUSCLE CONTRACTION IN THE LOWER BACK. HOLD THIS EXERCISE 10-20 SECONDS TWO OR THREE TIMES

WHILE STANDING, THE COMRADE NEEDS TO CROSS ONE ARM ACROSS THE CHEST AND ADD PRESSURE WITH THE OTHER ARM ON THE ELBOW. THE STRETCH SHOULD BE HELD FOR ROUGHLY 20-30 SECONDS ON EACH SIDE.

THE STANDARD SHOULDER STRETCH

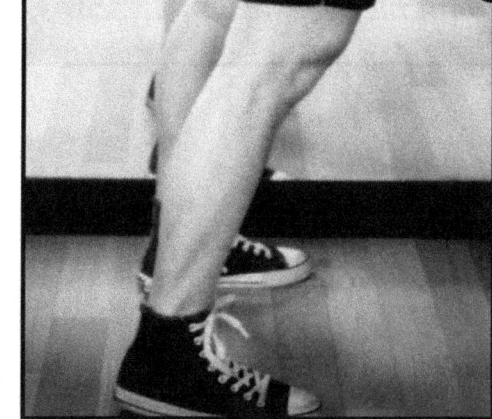

TO PERFORM THIS STRETCH, THE COMRADE WILL NEED A POST, POLL OR A WALL. WHILE PRESSING THE EXTENDED HAND AGAINST THE WALL, TURN THE BODY AWAY AND STRETCH THE CHEST. HOLD THE STRETCH FOR 20-30 SECONDS ON EACH SIDE.

THE STANDARD CHEST STRETCH

STANDARD BACK STRETCH

THIS IS A COMRADE FAVORITE STRETCH BECAUSE IT NOT ONLY STRETCHES THE BACK BUT FEELS GREAT TOO. THIS STRETCH REQUIRES A POST, POLL, RAIL OR STURDY PIECE OF GYM EQUIPMENT THAT CAN SUPPORT THE COMRADE'S WEIGHT. FIRST, GRAB THE POLE WITH ONE OR BOTH HANDS, BEND THE KNEES AND LEAN BACK WHILE HOLDING ON. KEEP BOTH HANDS EXTENDED AND SLIGHTLY LEAN THE HEAD FORWARD. HOLD THE STRETCH FOR 15-20 SECONDS WITH THE LEFT, RIGHT AND BOTH ARMS.

Fourth

If training in the gym, the first set of repetitions for a selected exercise should be performed slowly and executed through a full range of motion. Keep the weight light.

If training outside the gym, the same principal as above applies to all exercises after stretching and a light warm up is completed.

Example: Bench press. Start out by just pressing the bar without any added weight. Slowly take the bar up and down 10-15 times. The Comrade should feel his triceps and chest going through a deep stretch.

Specific Training Philosophies

Strength and Power

If a Comrade is interested in strength and power gain, the following illustration shows the approach toward that specific training philosophy.

Powerlifting

3 repetitions

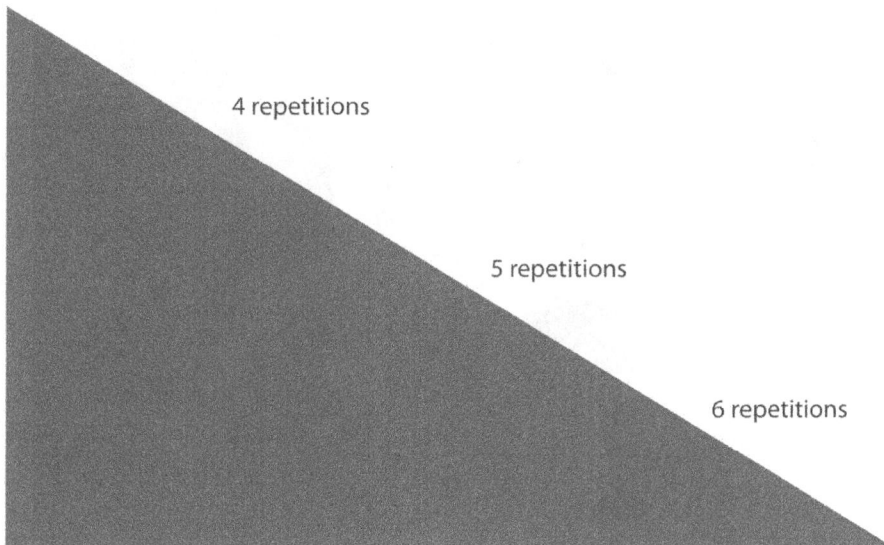

4 repetitions

5 repetitions

6 repetitions

Training for Strenghth and Power
Rest time 3-6 minutes between each set

Upon selecting a specific exercise like the bench press, squat or dead lift, the traditional approach is to lift as much weight as possible safely and properly 3 to 6 times per set. After performing the lift, a rest period of 3-6 minutes is considered to be standard rest time. It's highly recommended that a competent spotter is present along side when this type of training is performed.

If you decide to train primarily in the 3-6 repetition zone per set with extremely heavy weight for a long time, your body might morph to look something like the body image in the picture below. This is to provide you an idea of what may occur if you don't care about the ripped look. As a powerlifter, eating more food and pushing more weight is standard training practice.

POWER LIFTING PHILOSOPHY 3-6 REPS

(Notes)
- Over all a bulky look
- Very strong and powerful
- Important to incorporate cardiovascular activity to maintain a healthy heart .
- Important to eat food of value, but no specific strict diet is set .
- Important not to hold the breath on any heavy lift.

(Note) Many Comrades who wish to become bodybuilders but don't have the discipline to eat a clean diet end up looking like powerlifters.

If a Comrade is interested in muscle growth (hypertrophy), the following illustration addresses the approach toward that specific training philosophy.

Bodybuilding

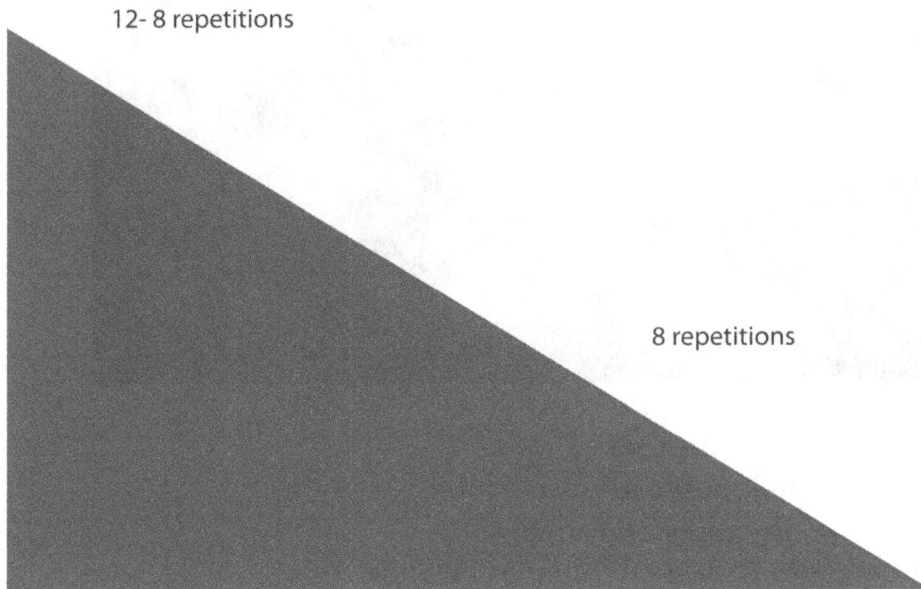

12- 8 repetitions

8 repetitions

Training for Muscle Growth (Hypertrophy)
Rest time 1-2 minutes between each set

Upon selecting a specific exercise, a moderately heavy weight is used. For example, a Comrade decides to do four sets for the bench press. He or she should be able to lift a moderately heavy weight (8-12 times in one set) almost failing or actually failing on the last repetition of each set. If training till failure on each set, a competent spotter is required.

If you decide to train primarily in the 8-12 repetition zone with moderately heavy weights for a long period of time, with proper diet this is something what the end result might look like.

(Notes)

- Ripped muscular overall look
- Requires a clean diet
- Requires a dedicated training schedule
- Requires organization
- By far one of the hardest but most rewarding training philosophies

If a Comrade is interested in endurance and/or weight loss, the following illustration addresses the approach toward that specific training philosophy.

Endurance and weight loss

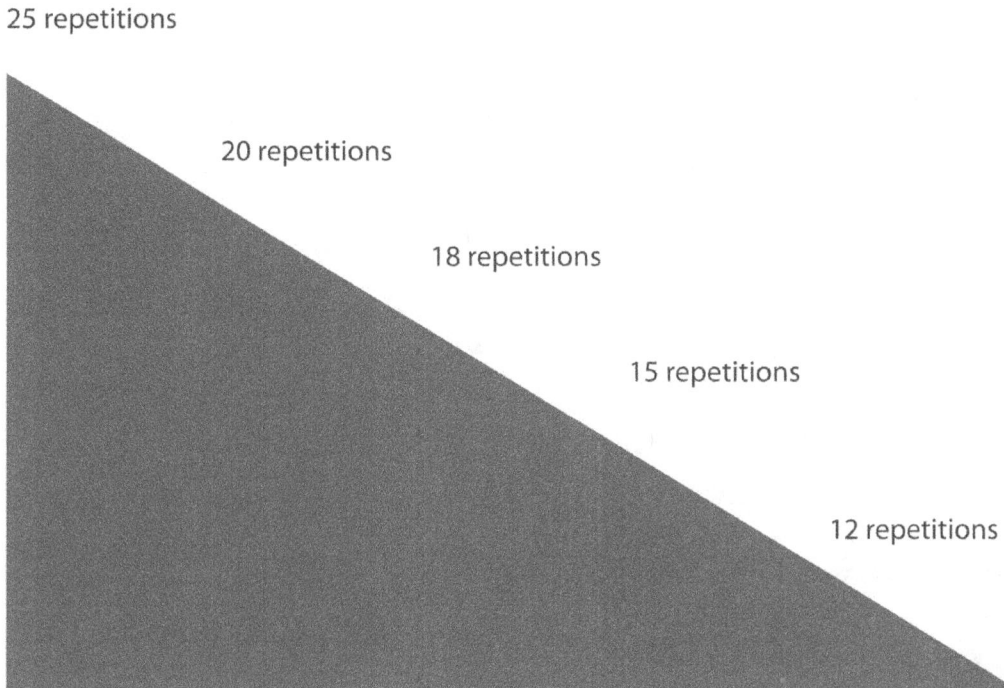

25 repetitions

20 repetitions

18 repetitions

15 repetitions

12 repetitions

Endurance and weight loss
Rest time 1 minute or less between each set

Upon selecting a specific exercise or a combination of exercises, the Comrade utilizes a light to moderate-light weight. The exercises are performed with high intensity, full range of motion and proper execution. The Russian Ripped philosophy is heavily influenced by this particular high rep approach.

If you decide to train primarily in the 20-25 repetition zone with light to light moderate weight for a long period of time, this is something what a Comrade might look like. This look resembles the dominant Russian Ripped image goal.

**ENDURANCE AND WEIGHT LOSS PHILOSOPHY
20-25 REPS PER SET 15-20 SETS**

(Notes)

- Very lean model like look
- Intensive light resistance training
- Lots of running and Stairmaster

The following training philosophy is highly unorthodox and militaristic. In this training approach, the overall performance aspect is focused on first, not the image. However, because the training is so intense, a good solid cage fighter like image is the usual result. If you choose to follow this unusual military training philosophy for a long period of time, you might look something like this:

UNORTHODOX MILITARY TRAINING PHILOSOPHY

(Notes)

- Performance (running, fighting, endurance, lifting)
- Not a lean look but an overall powerful image
- This is the (Soviet Russian badass training) philosophy

Chapter 9 - Mighty Chest Basics

This chapter focuses on specific selected chest exercises utilized by the Soviet Russian peoples of the glorious motherland. A Comrade might notice that the exercises performed are dominantly raw, free weight exercises. The Russian Ripped philosophy tries to stay away from machines and cables to ensure that the assistor muscles are also involved in the exercises. Good results may be attained by using guided non free weight machines, but from experience I can confidently state that "free weights provide better results for those Comrades who are in good enough condition to use them".

Bench Press (Including flat, incline and decline angles)

The glorious bench press is the standard two plate 225lbs minimum exercise all Russian Soviet children must properly submit to their parents at the age of 8. A powerful chest supported by superb triceps is what the bench press targets.

(Notes from the underground)

- Do not bounce the bar off the chest in a spasm like motion.
- If the elbows are buckling at the top and the Comrade slightly locks out before taking the weight down, he or she is probably lifting to fast. Throwing the weight up instead of press it up is wrong.
- Do not overload the weight on the Olympic bar to have some random Comrades charge to your aid when the weight is crushing down on your chest. Use a spotter when lifting heavy.
- Be sure to exhale when pressing the weigh up.
- Squeeze the chest when pressing the weight up.
- Get a full stretch when taking the weight down.
- Control the weight on the way down.

WIDE GRIP

THE WIDE GRIP STRESSES AND STRETCHES THE CHEST FARTHER THAN THE STANDARD GRIP.

STANDARD GRIP

THE STANDARD GRIP STRESSES THE CHEST AND TRICEPS.

- The glorious bench press approach uses the free bench press, not the railed smith machine. Free weight requires other muscles to kick in and stabilize the weight. This only applies to healthy Comrades without injuries.
- Joint flexibility and weight dictates how far a Comrade can lower the bar down towards the chest with control. If a Comrade has excellent range of motion and can safely bring down 100 lbs without pain to the chest and press it back up, same principal is to be applied for a heavier weight. If the Comrade can't complete the full range of motion on a heavy set, the weight is too heavy. It's time to back off. Full range of motion takes priority over heavy weight training every day of the week.

Standard Flat Bench Press

1. Lift the bar and hover it directly over the mid chest area with arms extended but not locked out.

2. Slowly inhale as you lower the weight down to about an inch above the chest in a slow, controlled manner. It's optional to slightly touch the chest if the Comrade is flexible enough to do so.

3. Pause for half a second and feel the stretch.

4. Exhale as you press the weight up in a controlled manner.

5. Squeeze the chest as the weight is lifted back to the highest point.

6. Keep a slight elbow angle at the top and do not lock the arms out.

FLAT BENCH PRESS

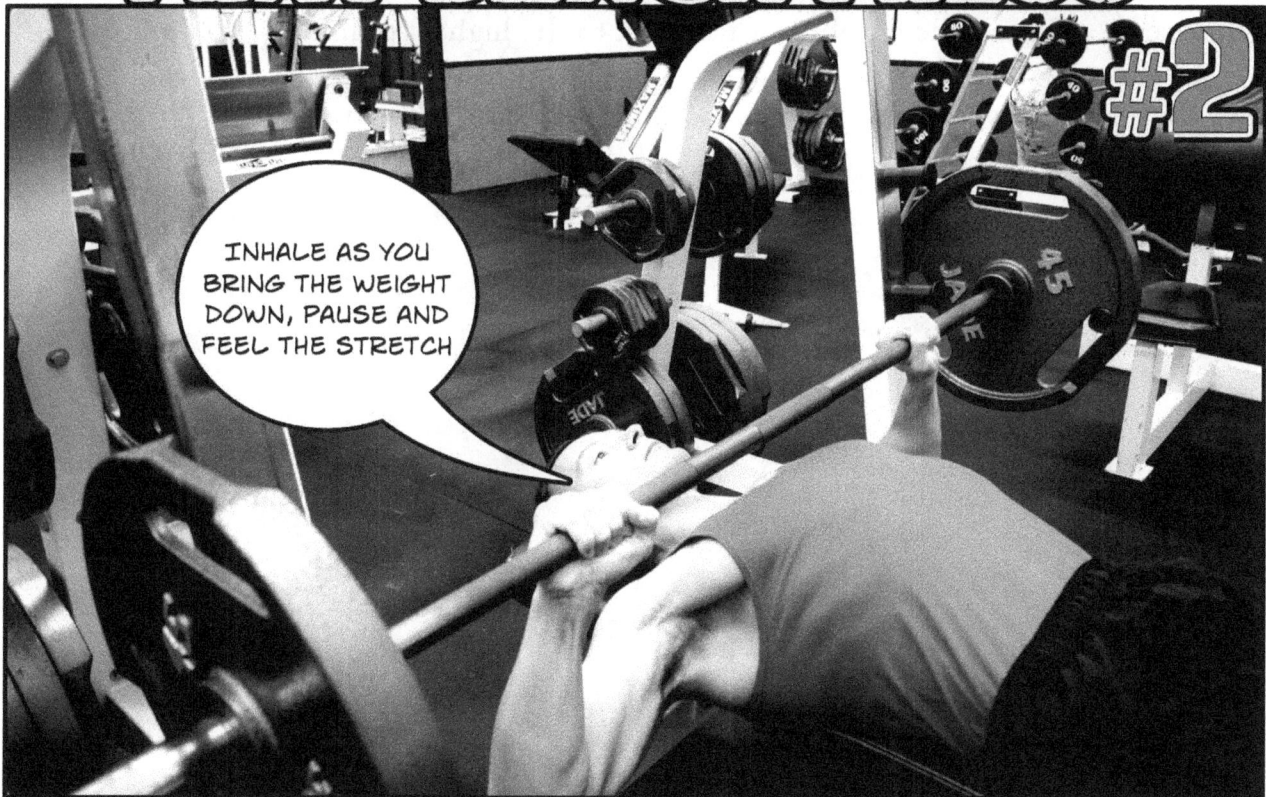

Incline Bench Press

The Incline bench press is almost a complete copy of the flat bench press except the movement is executed on an incline angled bench. For many Comrades, this is a more strenuous exercise because it's either neglected or executed immediately after the flat bench press when the chest is already fatigued.

(Note) Giving it your all on the flat bench press saps strength form the incline bench press. Every once in a while start with the incline bench press instead of the regular bench press as the first exercise.

The focus of this exercise is on the mid and upper chest. The triceps get attention as well. After acquiring a sturdy feel for this exercise, try lifting the mid back slightly off the pad. This creates an arc and lifts the chest slightly higher. Not all Comrades like doing this, but if executed properly, a deeper muscle stretch is felt when the bar comes down towards the chest.

1. Lift the bar and hover it directly over the mid chest area with arms extended but not locked out.

2. Slowly inhale as you lower the bar down to about an inch above the chest with control.

3. Pause for half a second and feel the stretch.

4. Exhale as you push the weight up in a controlled manner.

5. Squeeze the chest as the weight is lifted back to the highest point.

6. Keep a slight elbow angle at the top and do not lock out the arms.

STANDARD NON-ARCHED POSITION

ARCHED POSITION

HEY COMRADE! YOU CAN ACHIEVE A DEEPER CHEST STRETCH BY ARCHING THE BACK.

Decline Bench Press

This exercise is almost a complete copy of the flat bench press except the movement is executed on a decline angle. The focus is on the middle and lower chest. The triceps get attention as well. Many Comrades feel like their blood pressure goes through the roof when this exercise is performed. (Remember to exhale when pressing the weight up and do not strain the neck. Keep the neck down on the pad). If the Comrade decides to do this exercise, he or she should start with lightweight.

(Note) If you have a history of high blood pressure and it feels like your head is pounding simply lying down on a decline angle, then this is not the exercise for you.

1. Lift the bar and hover it directly over the mid chest area with arms extended but not locked out.

2. Slowly inhale as you lower the bar down to about an inch above the chest with control.

3. Pause for half a second and feel the stretch.

4. As you exhale press the weight up in a controlled manner.

5. Squeeze the chest as the weight is lifted back up to the highest point.

6. Keep a slight elbow angle at the top and do not lock out the arms.

STARTING POSITION
#1
DECLINE BENCH PRESS

#2
KEEP THE HEAD DOWN ON THE PAD TO AVOID A NECK STRAIN.

Dumbbell Press (Including flat, incline and decline angles)

The dumbbell flat bench press is very similar to the regular bench press with the addition of a fun balancing act and a farther range of motion for some. Because the Comrade doesn't have the bar directly over the chest, he or she can take the dumbbells farther down for a better stretch. The focus of the flat dumbbell press is on the mid chest area. The triceps get attention as well. In Glorious Soviet Motherland Russia all grandmothers can press 100 lb dumbbells in each hand at the same time with ease. If they can not, then they are considered to be unacceptable grandmothers.

(Notes from the underground)

• Always start with lightweight to ensure the balancing of the dumbbells feels comfortable. Comrades who have no experience doing this exercise may need to take some time and adapt to it. With time, stabilization becomes easier as the body naturally adapts to the exercise.
• Be sure to inhale as the weight is brought down.
• Control the weight on the way down.
• Get a full stretch at the bottom and pause for a split second.
• Be sure to exhale when pressing the weigh up.
• Squeeze the chest when pressing the dumbbells back up.
• Control the weight on the way up.
• If the Comrade uses heavy weight, it's necessary to have a competent spotter who pays attention. For the love of all that is holy if you do not use the assistance of a spotter and drop the dumbbells on the floor do not hold on to them. However, if someone is standing behind you or near you and the dumbbells fall on that lucky person, he or she will not have a glorious day. Be aware of the surroundings and use a spotter!
• Always double check to ensure that the same amount of weight is in each hand. Sometimes 5 pounds more in one hand than the other may result in an injury.

(**Note**) Dumbbell weight mix-ups occur typically due to lack of attention.

1. Select two dumbbells that weigh the same amount for each hand.

2. Sit down on the bench and place the dumbbells on the knees carefully.

3. With control slowly roll back.

4. Place the legs on the ground.

5. Lift the dumbbells while exhaling and hover them directly over the mid chest area.

6. Slowly inhale as you lower the dumbbells down to the sides of the chest.

7. Pause for half a second and feel the stretch.

8.   Exhale as you press the dumbbells up in a controlled manner.

9.   Squeeze the chest together as the dumbbells are pushed up to the highest point.

10. Keep a slight elbow angle at the top and do not lock out the arms. (It's optional to touch the dumbbells together at the top).

11. Upon completing the set, turn the dumbbells parallel to each other, bring the knees up to the dumbbells and propel the body in a forward motion with the dumbbells placed on the knees.

12. The forward weight shift pushes the Comrade forward and allows him, or her to stand up or sit up.

13. Warning, the more weight a Comrade decides to use, the faster he or she will shoot forward. Be sure that no one is walking in the front when the dismount is executed.
I have witnessed a Comrade once shoot his body forward without checking for other Comrades. At that exact moment another Comrade was walking by. Long story short, both Comrades ended up in the mirror.

#1 — STARTING POSITION

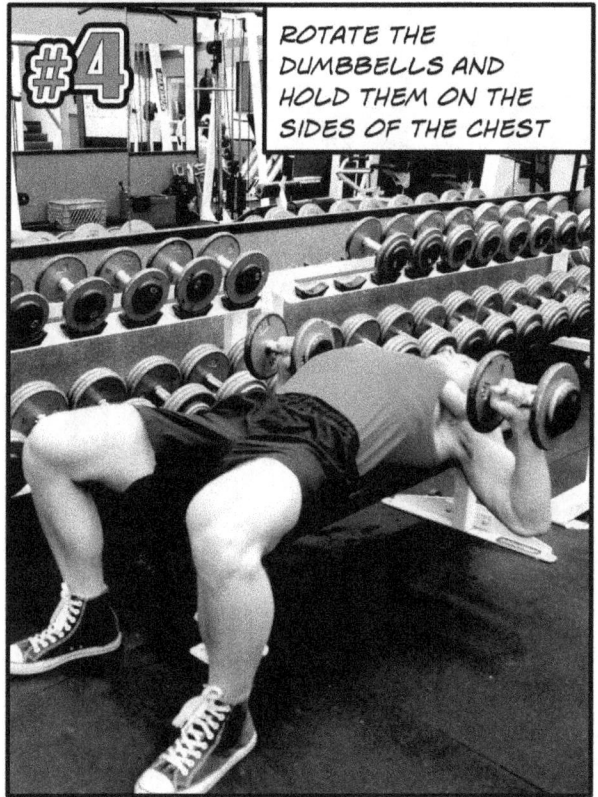
#2 — ROLL BACK WITH CONTROL

DUMBBELL PRESS

#3 — PLACE THE LEGS DOWN ON THE GROUND AND KEEP THE DUMBBELLS PARALLEL TO EACH OTHER

#4 — ROTATE THE DUMBBELLS AND HOLD THEM ON THE SIDES OF THE CHEST

Incline Dumbbell Press

One thing to keep in mind on the incline dumbbell press Comrade is that you are training middle and upper chest. Not the shoulders. It's a must to find a proper incline angle that works best around the 45 degree mark. If the Comrade feels like he or she is using shoulders heavily on this exercise then the bench angle should be lowered. Going high on the incline angle makes the exercise a dumbbell military press which (works the shoulders). Shoulder training is included in another chapter. The focus of this exercise is on the mid and upper chest area. The triceps get attention as well. After acquiring a solid feel for the incline dumbbell press, the Comrade can try lifting the mid back slightly off the pad. Not all Comrades like doing this, but if executed properly, a deeper muscle stretch is felt when the weight is brought down towards the chest.

1.   Select two dumbbells that weigh the same amount for each hand.

2.   Sit down on the adjusted incline bench and place the dumbbells on the knees carefully.

3.   Place the back on the pad, with control kick the dumbbells up towards the chest and stabilize them.

4. As you exhale, lift the dumbbells and hover them directly over the mid chest area.

5.   Slowly inhale as you lower the weights down to the sides of the chest.

6.   Pause for half a second and feel the stretch.

7.   Exhale as you press the dumbbells up in a controlled manner.

8.   Squeeze the chest together as the weights are pushed to the highest point.

9.   Keep a slight elbow angle at the top and do not lock out the arms. (It's optional to touch the dumbbells together at the top).

10. Upon completing the set, kick the knees up and place the dumbbells on the knees.

11. The weight shift will push the Comrade forward and allow him or her to stand up or sit up.

12. Warning, the more weight a Comrade decides to use, the faster he or she will shoot forward. Be sure that no one is walking in front of you when the dismount is executed.

#1

BASICALLY COMRADE, THE INCLINE DUMBBELL PRESS IS A COPY OF THE REGULAR DUMBBELL PRESS EXCEPT IT'S EXECUTED ON AN ANGLE. IF YOU FEEL LIKE YOU ARE USING THE SHOULDERS EXTENSIVELY ON THIS EXERCISE, LOWER THE ANGLE OF THE BENCH.

INCLINE DUMBBELL PRESS

#2

IF THE WEIGHT IS HEAVY, KICKING IT UP HELPS TO GET IT INTO POSITION. IT'S A GOOD IDEA TO GET INTO A HABIT OF USING THIS TECHNIQUE.

USE THE LEGS TO HELP KICK UP THE WEIGHT

#3

PLACE THE LEGS ON THE GROUND AND STABILIZE THE DUMBBELLS

#4

ROTATE THE DUMBELLS OUT AND BRING THEM TO THE SIDES OF THE CHEST

#5

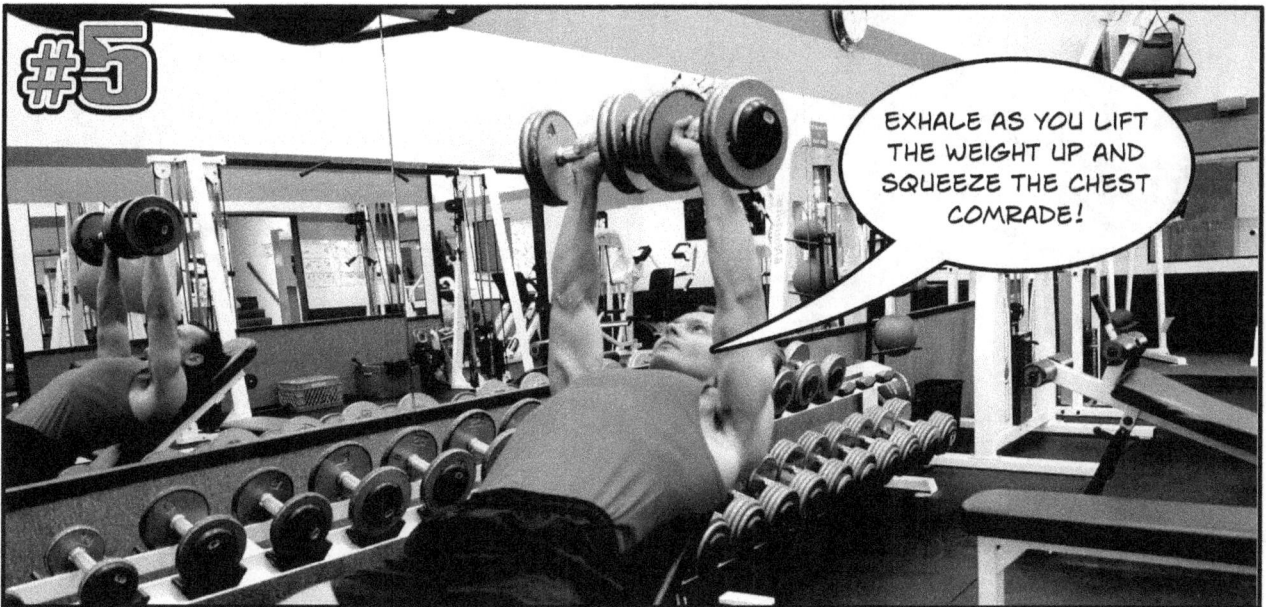

EXHALE AS YOU LIFT THE WEIGHT UP AND SQUEEZE THE CHEST COMRADE!

TO DISMOUNT: BRING THE DUMBBELLS DOWN TO THE CHEST. KEEP THEM PARALLEL TO EACH OTHER. KICK THE LEGS UP, PLACE THE DUMBBELLS ON THE KNEES AND ROLL FORWARD.

Decline Dumbbell Press

The focus of the decline dumbbell press is on the middle and lower chest. The triceps get attention as well. Many Comrades feel like their blood pressure goes through the roof when this exercise is performed.

(Note) Unlike the decline bench press this exercise receives fewer complaints from Comrades who have high blood pressure, however caution should still be implemented.

1. Select two dumbbells that weigh the same amount for each hand.

2. Sit down on the adjusted decline bench, fasten the legs firmly under the leg pad and place the dumbbells on the knees carefully. It is recommended to have a competent spotter for this exercise.

3. With control, lean back holding the dumbbells parallel to each other. (Do not strain the abdominals). Stabilize the dumbbells and bring them slowly to the sides of the chest.

4. Exhale while lifting the dumbbells up and hover them directly over the mid chest area.

5. Slowly inhale as you lower the dumbbells down towards the chest with control.

6. Pause for half a second and feel a deep stretch at the bottom.

7. Exhale as you press the dumbbells up with control.

8. Squeeze the chest together as the weights are pressed to the highest point.

9. Keep a slight elbow angle at the top and do not lock out the arms.

10. Upon completing the exercise, due to the decline angle, it may be difficult to sit up with the dumbbells. If that is the case, drop the dumbbells on the ground. **(Note)** Some gyms might frown upon that, but if you are training unusually heavy without a spotter and can't continue, you run out of other options.

DECLINE DUMBBELL PRESS

TURN THE
DUMBBELLS OUT AND
PLACE THEM ON THE
SIDES OF THE CHEST

EXHALE WHILE
PRESSING THE
DUMBBELLS UP AND
SQUEEZE THE CHEST

TO DISMOUNT: BRING THE DUMBBELLS DOWN TO THE SIDES OF THE CHEST AND DROP THEM ON THE GROUND.

COMRADE! IT'S VERY CONVENIENT TO DROP THE WEIGHTS INSTEAD OF CRUNCHING BACK UP WITH THEM.

Dumbbell Flys (Flat bench flyes and incline bench flys)

An excellent exercise that stretches the chest is known as 'the Glorious Dumbbell Flys. Like the bench press exercises, the three main versions of this exercise can be performed on an incline, decline and regular flat benches. We will primarily focus on the flat and incline dumbbell flies. The Soviet Russians call this exercise "I am not a fly , but I fly."

(Notes from the underground)

•   Always start with lightweight to ensure you have stability while going through the full range of motion. Comrades who have no experience with this exercise may need to take some time and adjust by starting slow.

•   Inhale when the dumbbells are brought down.

•   Get a full stretch at the bottom.

•   Exhale when taking the dumbbells back up.

•   Squeeze the chest as you fly-squeeze up.

•   Control the weight.

•   When using heavy weight, it's important that the Comrade has a competent spotter who pays attention.

•   Always double check to ensure you are using the same amount of weight in both hands. Five pounds more in one hand over the other may result in an injury.

1.   Select two dumbbells that weigh the same amount for each hand.

2.   Sit down on the bench and place the dumbbells carefully on the knees.

3.   With control roll back.

4.   Place the legs on the ground.

5.   Lift the dumbbells up and hover them parallel to each other over the mid chest area.

6.   Slowly inhale as you lower the dumbbells down to the sides of the chest with arms extended and slightly bent at the elbows.

7.   Pause for half a second and feel the stretch.

8.   Exhale and push-fly the dumbbells up in a controlled manner.

9.   Squeeze the chest together as the dumbbells come up to the highest point.

10. Keep a slight elbow angle at the top and do not lock out the arms.

11. Upon completing the set, bring the knees up, place the dumbbells on the knees and propel the body in a forward motion to sit or stand up.

#1 STARTING POSITION

DUMBBELL FLYS

#2 ROLL BACK WITH THE DUMBBELLS

#3 — PLACE THE LEGS ON THE GROUND AND INHALE

#4 — EXHALE AND LIFT THE DUMBBELLS STRAIGHT UP

#5

INHALE, STRETCH THE CHEST AND PAUSE FOR A SPLIT SECOND

#6

ON THE EXHALE, LIFT-FLY THE DUMBBELLS TO THE TOP AND CONTRACT THE CHEST

#7

TO DISMOUNT: LIFT THE LEGS UP AND PLACE THE DUMBBELLS ON THE KNEES

#8

ROLL FORWARD WITH CONTROL AND STAND UP

Incline Dumbbell Flys

The incline dumbbell flies primarily focus on the mid and upper chest area. In Soviet Russia we call this exercise "Bear Hug."

1. Select two dumbbells that weigh the same amount for each hand.

2. Sit down on the bench and place the dumbbells carefully on the knees.

3. With control roll back.

4. Place the legs on the ground.

5. Lift the dumbbells and hover them parallel to each other over the mid chest area.

6. As you inhale, slowly bring the dumbbells down to the sides of the chest with arms extended and slightly bent at the elbows.

7. Pause for half a second and feel the stretch.

8. Exhale and push-fly the dumbbells up in a controlled manner.

9. Squeeze the chest together as the dumbbells come up to the highest point.

10. Keep a slight elbow angle at the top and do not lock out the arms.

11. Upon completing the set, bring the knees up, place the dumbbells on the knees and propel the body in a forward motion to sit or stand up.

STARTING POSITION

INCLINE DUMBBELL FLYS

ROLL BACK WITH THE DUMBBELLS

PLACE THE LEGS ON THE GROUND AND POSITION THE DUMBBELLS OVER THE CHEST

INHALE AND BRING THE ARMS DOWN. PAUSE AT THE BOTTOM AND FEEL A GOOD STRETCH.

EXHALE, BRING THE ARMS BACK UP AND SQUEEZE THE CHEST

TO DISMOUNT: BRING THE KNEES UP, PLACE THE DUMBBELLS ON THE KNEES AND SHIFT THE BODY WEIGHT FORWARD

This concludes the chapter on mighty chest training Comrade. Yes, there are many other types of chest exercises available on the open market. The reason we covered these specific exercises is because they are the fundamental basics that get the job done. Many Comrades try to train fancy and stray from the foundation upon which the glorious chest is built.

A reminder from the Polite Bureau: Remember Comrades. Monday is international chest day. So train chest some other day.

Bear walk into a bar with flexed chest.
Bartender say "Why you flex chest?"
Bear look at bartender and yell to everyone "GET THAT SPY!"
In Soviet Russia chest flex you and all true Russians know that!
Word!

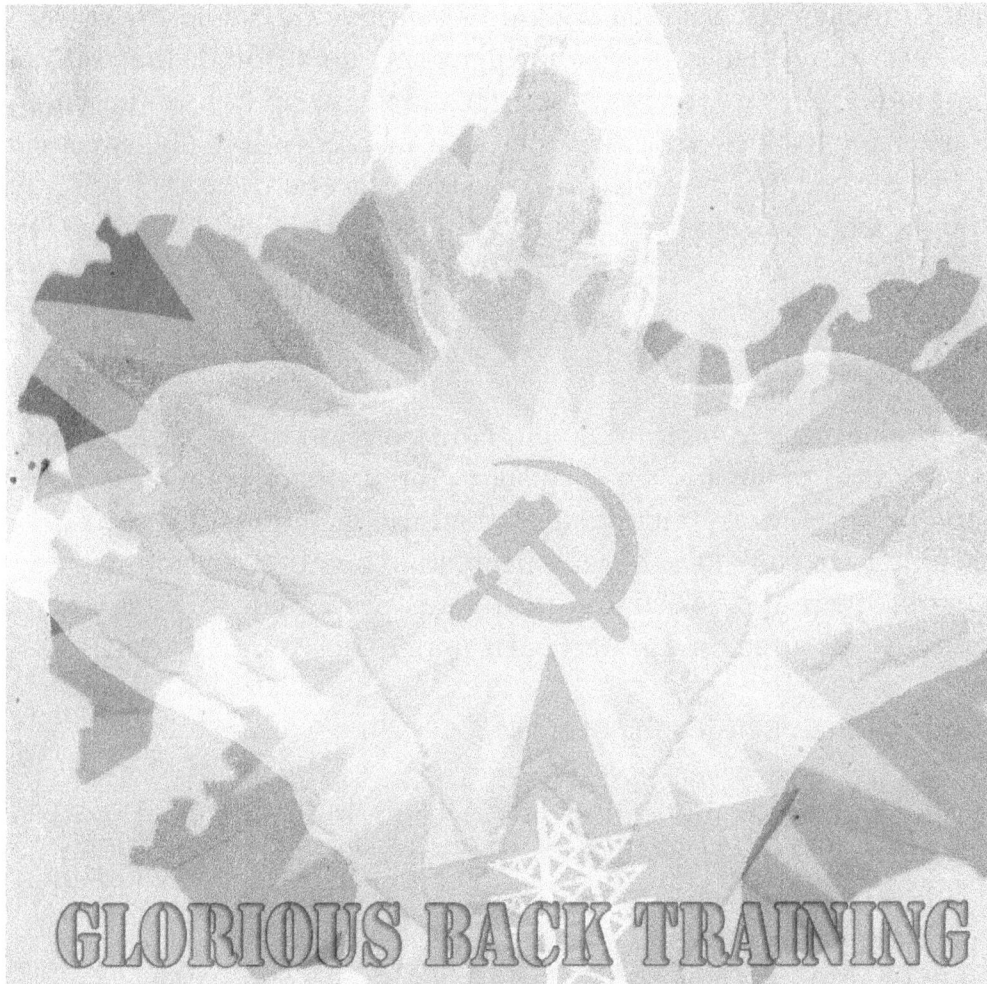
GLORIOUS BACK TRAINING

Chapter 10 - Mighty Back

Glorious back Comrade! All Comrades who train back in the Soviet motherland live a healthy upright life. However, a strong back isn't just apt for a trouble free posture; it's also convenient for plowing potato fields when the horse or tractor needs a break.

If the back is trained properly, a V shaped taper has a tendency to develop over time. This makes the waist look smaller. A properly built wide back also fills in the clothes much better giving a Comrade sexy bonus points.

Back Basics
Notes form the underground

• Building the back is difficult yet rewarding. Comrades should not neglect proper back training. Many Comrades do not push themselves hard enough on back training and have a tendency to just go through the motions of easy back exercises.

• Every Comrade should try and transition from (Wide Grip Lat Pulldowns & V Handle Pulldowns) to (Wide Grip Pullups & Close Grip Chinups).

• In the world of today back pain speaks loudly to many Comrades. If you have a bad back, for the love of everything that is holy, train light and go through the full range of motion slowly to prevent injury. Be sure to always stretch and warm up before training.

• Yes, there are many back exercises on the open market today. The specific back exercises in this chapter are selected, because they are considered to be the core back building exercises deemed by the Soviet Russian generals of the secret Back Training High Command University.

Back
Wide Grip Lat Pulldowns

The wide grip lat pulldown exercise is a downgraded version of the wide grip pullup. Usually Comrades can't perform pullups when they start glorious back training in the initial phase of training. With minor differences, both exercise focus on widening the lats (sides of the back). Follow the directions carefully to achieve a deep stretch and contraction on every repetition. Some may disagree with the execution technique presented for this exercise. In Soviet motherland Russia we all agree on this particular upper back training approach.

1. Select a comfortable weight for the exercise.

2. Sit comfortably and adjust the leg padding over the thighs to hold down the legs before beginning the exercise.

3. Stand up, grab the bar as wide and comfortably as you can.

4. With arms extended, holding the bar, slowly sit back down into the seat and place the legs underneath the pad.

5. Stretch and slightly lean forward.

6. Exhale as you bring the bar down towards the chest.

7. Be sure to arch the back with the chest slightly pointing up.

8. Pause for half a second at the bottom and contract the back.

9. Inhale as you come back up with control to full arm extension.

10. Slightly lean forward for a full stretch and repeat the steps.

#3

BRING THE BAR DOWN TOWARDS THE CHEST AND PAUSE. FEEL THE BACK MUSCLES CONTRACT.

Wide Grip Pullups

(Note) It's better to do 3 sets of 3 full range wide grip pullups than 3 or 4 sets of 10 half @$$ pullup repetitions. As the Comrade builds strength over time and drops fat weight, he or she will be able to perform proper pullups. The key to pullup progression, is persistence and patience.

1. For the Comrades who are not as tall as other Comrades be sure to have a bench or a box on the side to help you reach the bar.

2. After grabbing the bar, the Comrade is to hang all the way down and let the body weight pull him or her completely down for a good back stretch.

3. Do not swing or kick yourself up. There are some new fun training philosophies out on the market, but for this exercise you are to follow Russian Ripped philosophy which requires full control, concentration and proper old school technique.

4. Exhale on the way up and try to bring the chest toward the pullup bar while slightly arching the back.

5. Do the best you can to pause for half a second at the top and contract the back muscles.

6. Inhale on the way down.

7. Come down entirely, pause and feel a deep back stretch.

WIDE GRIP PULLUPS

#1 STARTING POSITION

#2

NEVER, NEVER, NEVER GIVE UP! IF YOU CAN'T DO ANY PULLUPS, GET YOUR BUTT ON THE BAR AND HOLD THE CONTRACTED POSITION AS LONG AS YOU CAN.

IT'S BETTER TO STRUGGLE FOR A YEAR AND DO ONLY ONE PULLUP RATHER THAN TO NEVER DO A PULLUP AT ALL.

Close Grip Lat Pulldowns (V handle)

The close grip lat pulldowns with the V handle mostly works the lats (sides of the back). If executed correctly, the Comrade also feels an igniting feeling of small muscles being activated along the spine.

(Note) The more a Comrade emphasizes on arching the back when taking the V handle down towards the chest, the more muscles along the spine will contract. The spinal muscle activation starts from the central spine area and extends downward towards the lower back (Erector Spinae).

1. Select a comfortable weight for the exercise.

2. Sit comfortably and adjust the leg padding over the thighs to hold down the legs comfortably before beginning the exercise.

3. Stand up and get a firm grip on the V handle.

4. With arms extended holding the V handle, slowly sit back down in the seat and place the legs underneath the pad.

5. Stretch and slightly lean forward.

6. As you exhale bringing the V bar down towards the chest.

7. Be sure to arch the back keeping the chest pointing in the upwards direction.

8. Pause for half a second at the bottom and contract the back.

9. Inhale when coming back up with control to full arm extension.

10. Slightly lean forward for a full stretch and repeat the steps.

#1 STARTING POSITION

#2 ENDING POSITION

CLOSE GRIP LAT PULLDOWNS

Close Grip Chinups

Yes Comrade, this is a tremendously difficult exercise. However, if a Comrade is dropping unwanted fat weight and builds over all body strength, with time this exercise becomes reasonable.

(Note) If a Comrade can't perform this exercise, it's suggested that he or she try holding the contracted position at the top as long as possible and then slowly lower the body down with control.

1.   For the Comrades who are not as tall as other Comrades, be sure to have a bench or a box on the side to help reach the bar.

2.   After grabbing the V handle and placing it on the pullup bar, the Comrade is to hang all the way down while holding on the V handle with both hands.

3.   Do not swing or kick the legs or hips to gain upward momentum.

4.   Exhale while pulling the body up and arch the back to elevate the chest.

5.   Try to pause for half a second at the top.

6.   Slowly inhale as you come entirely back down for a full stretch.

CLOSE GRIP CHINUPS

T- Bar Row

Put some quality mass on your back with this exercise Comrade! In Soviet Russia we call this exercise (The Drunken Wife). Pretend you have a wife, and she has fallen on the ground. Every time you pick her up she falls down again. Ladies you can call this exercise (The Drunken Husband). But all kidding aside, this is a remarkably effective exercise for the back.
(Note) If a Comrade feels that he or she is primarily working out the biceps or the legs when performing the t-bar row, it's a clear sign the Comrade should use less weight. It may also mean that the exercise is being executed incorrectly.

1. Place an Olympic 45lb bar at a 45 degree angle with one end of the bar in the wall corner.

2. Slide some weight on the bar opposite side of the wall.

3. Grab the V handle with both hands and lock yourself in behind the weight.

4. Keep the lower back tight, do not round the back, slightly look up and push the chest out.

5. Exhale as you lift the bar towards the chest.

6. Pause at the top when the plate weight touches the chest area and contract the back.

7. As you inhale slowly lower the weight down.

8. Be sure to fully extend the arms to go through the full range of motion.

9. Do not slam the weight on the ground but do make slight contact by taping the ground with control. **(Note)** This ensures you are going through the full range of motion.

10. Be careful and always start out with a lightweight.

T- BAR ROW

SOME GYMS ARE EQUIPPED WITH SPECIAL METAL CORNERS SPECIFICALLY FOR THIS EXERCISE. THE METAL CORNER PROTECTS THE WALL FROM DAMAGE. IF THE METAL CORNER IS NOT TO BE FOUND, ASK THE GYM OWNER OR GYM STAFF IF IT'S OK TO DO THIS EXERCISE.

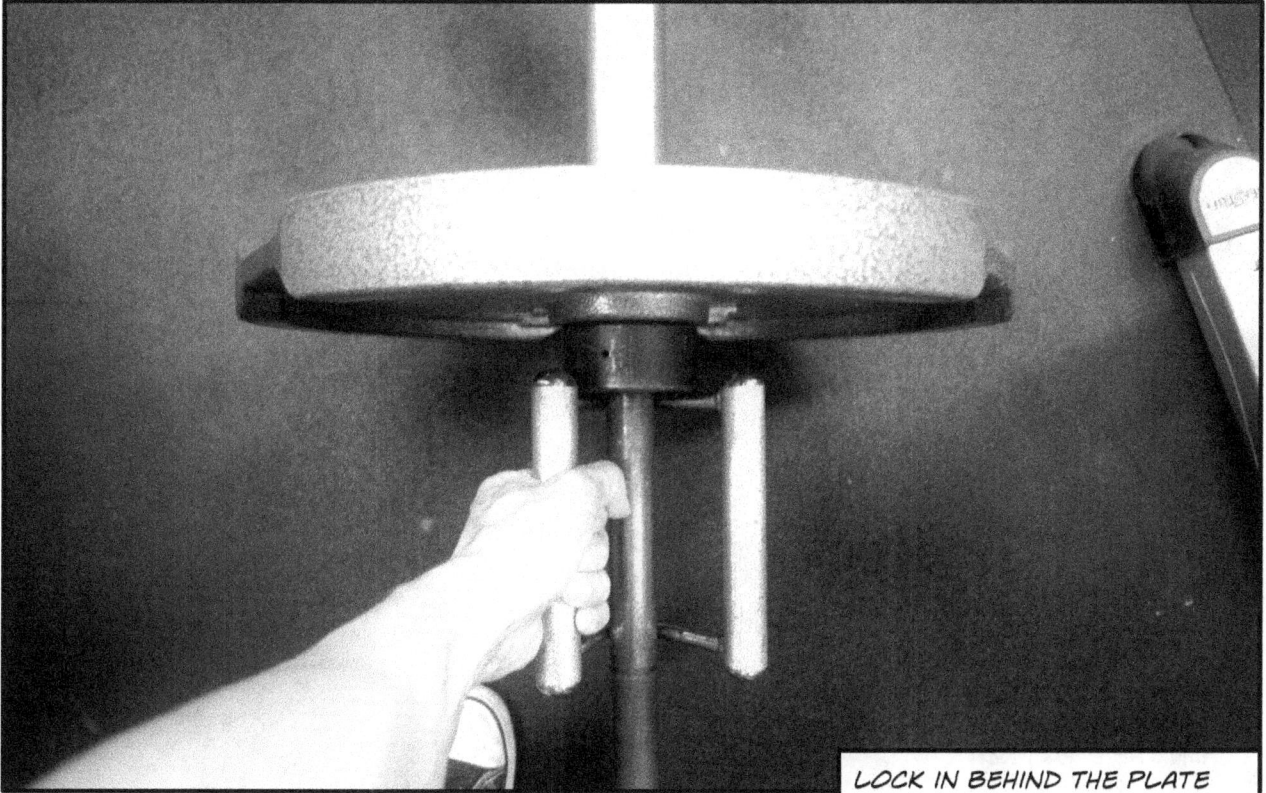

LOCK IN BEHIND THE PLATE WITH THE V-HANDLE. DO NOT ROUND THE BACK.

#1

PAUSE AT THE TOP

Wide Grip Cable Rows

The Wide Grip Cable Row is a standard Comrade exercise that should be a part of any primary back routine. A Comrade has the option of using several different grips and bars for this exercise. In Soviet motherland Russia we call this exercise "The Indestructo Boat Motor." Why? Because Soviet Russian people are so strong they can row a boat with one wooden paddle faster than a 100 horsepower motorboat and still kick Spartan @$$ all at the same time.

1. Attach a wide grip bar to the row machine. Take hold of the bar with a wide grip and place one foot on the front footing base.

2. Slowly sit back and place the other leg on the front footing base. Keep both legs slightly bent.

3. Inhale as you lean forward as far as possible with the weight pulling you forward.

4. While exhaling, pull the bar back towards the chest.

5. Pause for a second, feel the back muscles contract, inhale and lean forward again to full extension.

PLACE ONE LEG ON THE FRONT FOOTING PLATFORM AND SLIGHTLY LEAN BACK

WIDE GRIP CABLE ROWS

SIT DOWN ON THE BENCH

STARTING POSITION

#1

INHALE, LEAN FORWARD AND STRETCH THE BACK

#2

AS YOU EXHALE, PULL THE BAR BACK TOWARDS THE CHEST AND CONTRACT THE BACK

The Dead Lift

The Dead lift is one of the main exercises performed by powerlifters.

(Note) All though this exercise mainly focuses on the lower back the Comrade will feel his or her whole body at work.

(Note) In Soviet Russia we call this exercise the "Bear Lift." All the Comrades who want to become strong like bear, build a steel reinforced body frame like superhero and burn lots of calories should not just keep this exercise in mind, but actually do it.

(Note) Any Comrades who practice mixed martial arts should put this exercise on the favorites list.

1. Walk up to the bar and center yourself keeping the legs at about shoulder with apart.

2. Grab the bar a few inches away from where the shins are when standing in front of the bar.

3. The grip preference varies with individuals. Try gripping the bar with the left hand turned away from the body and the right hand turned towards the body.

4. As the Comrade prepares to lift the weight, he or she is not to round the back. The Comrade is to look forward, and keep the legs bent. **(Note)** Remember to exhale, DO NOT hold the breath when lifting the weight up.

5. Lift the weight up with control keeping the arms straight.

6. At the top, slightly lean back.

7. Lock the legs out and hold the weight for a split second while keeping the whole body tight.

8. When taking the weight back down, inhale and slightly start to bend the legs.

9. If performing multiple repetitions with light-moderate weight, slightly tap the plates on the ground before coming back up for the next repetition.

#1

STARTING POSITION

THE DEAD LIFT

#2

THE GRIP

#2

DO NOT ROUND THE BACK

#3

Lower Back Extensions

The purpose of this exercise is not to make the hamstrings burn, (the back of the legs). Unfortunately, Comrades who don't stretch or train hamstrings may feel some discomfort. This discomforting burning sensation should be a reminder to all Comrades that leg training is not to be skipped.

The purpose of this exercise is to build the lower back (the lower erector muscles).

In Soviet Russia we call this exercise "Water Out Of the Well".

(Note) Some fitness professionals will say that Comrades should not hyperextend the spine backwards as far as presented in the following illustration. However, a healthy Comrade who is warmed up and does not rush through the exercise can experience a glorious muscle contraction by slightly hyperextending the spine while maintaining control at all times.

1. First, the Comrade is to get on the bench facing down. (Depending on the bench type) He or she will lock the back of the legs on some sort of padding or slide the heels behind a metal strip located on the lower platform of the bench. Be sure the front padding is positioned comfortably on the thighs. Some Comrades do this exercise with the padding positioned in a terribly awkward position.

2. Slowly lower the upper body down and keep the arms positioned closely together. Let the elbows lead in the descending motion.

3. When coming up, exhale and slowly swing the arms back. Bring the shoulder blades towards each other. Pause at the top and squeeze the back. **(Note)** The Comrade will feel many muscles activated along the spine.

STARTING POSITION

LOWER BACK EXTENSIONS

IF YOU FEEL A BURN IN THE HAMSTRINGS (THE BACK OF THE LEGS), YOU MIGHT WANT TO WARM UP AND STRETCH LONGER BEFORE BEGINNING THE WORKOUT.

COMRADES WHO HAVE STRONG LEG POWER CAN LITERALLY "KICK ASS HARD"

LEG TRAINING

Chapter 11- Mighty Legs

Glorious Mighty Legs! Legs are perhaps the most neglected body part that Comrades avoid training. Why do Comrades avoid leg training? Any glorious Comrade, who has trained legs properly in the past, will tell you that walking or sitting down was somewhat discomforting afterwards.

(Note) Leg training is followed by discomforting muscle pain. This is one of the key reasons Comrades are not so enthusiastic about training legs.

(Note) Legs need just as much attention as other body parts.

Have you ever seen someone in the gym with a glorious looking upper body and no legs? I have. And sorry if I offend anyone in particular, but that is hilariously funny. If you are one of those lopsided Comrades who lacks leg power relax, take a breath, and for the love of everything that is holy please start training the legs.

Notes from the underground
• A number of fitness "professionals" will not agree with the way some of the exercises are demonstrated in this book and especially this chapter. They are entitled to their opinion.

- Remember that you need to stretch thoroughly and warm up before training legs.
- Always exhale on exertion.
- To have a well rounded physique, you need to train legs!

Soviet Squat

The Soviet squat is not the standard version of the squat. In the standard version of the squat, the Comrade only comes down to about a ninety degree angle without dropping the glorious butt past the knees. Standard fitness "professionals" agree that this is the safe and proper way of doing the standard squat. The Soviet squat steps outside that rule. In the Soviet squat the glorious behind makes contact with the calves. In the standard squat the primary focus is on the thighs. In the Soviet squat the focus is on the thighs and the (gluteus maximus) aka the glorious butt. For all those Comrades who wish to develop an outstanding round firm behind this is the ultimate exercise for doing just that.

(Note) Start off with lightweight or no weight. If the Comrade has limited flexibility he or she should work on proper balance and deep stretching to develop strong technique before attempting to do the Soviet squat with weight.

(Note) It's recommended to look slightly up at a fixed point when squatting down, this helps with balance.

1. Set the bar on the squat rack at a comfortable position before dismounting the bar. **(Note)** Try to use a squat rack with safety bars.

2. Dismount the bar from the rack and rest it on the upper back. At first, the exercise may feel discomforting. **(Note)** Some gyms offer round cushion pads that wrap around the bar to combat the discomforting feeling.

3. Keep the entire body tight and always stay in control of the weight. The natural leg positioning varies with all individuals. **(Note)** The normal leg position is keeping the legs at shoulder width apart and the toes pointing forward or just slightly angled out.

4. Slowly squat down and inhale through the nose keeping the bar centered on the shoulders. **(Note)** Leaning forward too much will strain the lower back. Keep an upright posture.

5. When contact is made between the calves and the gluteus maximus (butt), pause at the bottom for a split second.

6. As you exhale through the mouth, keep the abbs tight, squeeze the glutes (butt) and come up.

  (Note) The option to lock out the legs at the top varies with individual preference. If the Comrade decides to lock out at the top it's recommended flexing the thighs in an upward motion right after the lock out.

#1

STARTING POSITION

THE SOVIET SQUAT

Dumbbell Duck Squat

This exercise is directed toward all the beautiful Comrade ladies who want to build a nice firm butt, hamstrings and thighs. Please be sure to stretch before doing this exercise. **(Note)** At first perform the exercise without weight. The primary focus is to feel a deep burn in the thighs, hams and the (gluteus maximus) aka the glorious butt. A word to all male Comrades, do not skip this exercise.

1. Hold a dumbbell by the sides with both hands down the center of the body.

2. Place the legs far apart from each other with the toes pointing out.

3. Come down slowly and inhale until the dumbbell slightly taps the ground.

4. Come back up and exhale. **(Note)** Squeeze the mighty butt as hard as possible on the way up. If the butt or legs start to shake, that means you are pushing yourself. Good for you!

5. Lock the legs out at the top and flex the thighs.

DUMBBELL DUCK SQUAT

Leg Extensions

This is a hugely popular exercise among the bodybuilding crowd. The leg extensions develop the area around the knee and help promote the visible separation between the thigh muscles. Usually leg extensions are performed as a warm up exercise or a final finishing leg exercise. Depending on how a Comrade points his toes when lifting the legs, determines the angle from which the thigh muscle group is stimulated.

1. Sit down on the leg extension machine and set the pad to cover the lower shin area.

2. As you exhale and bring the weight up, pause at the top with the toes pointing straight up.

3. With control slowly lower the weight back down as you inhale.
(Note) Alternating the position of the toes when lifting the legs up is a terrific alternative to utilize. Switch up between pointing the toes up, inside and outside every few repetitions.

STARTING POSITION

LEG EXTENSIONS

THIS IS THE STANDARD LEG EXTENSION EXECUTION WITH THE TOES POINTING UP

STANDARD POSITIONING OF THE TOES

#3

TOES POINTING INWARD

TOES POINTING INWARD

#4

TOES POINTING OUTWARD

IF YOU WANT TO ACHIEVE GOOD THIGH SEPARATION, CHANGING UP THE TOE ANGLES AS YOU COME UP AND PAUSE IS HIGHLY RECOMMENDED

Hamstring Curls

The hamstring curls in Soviet Russia are known as Crane Pulls. When ever a tractor gets stuck in the mud or snow, all a Comrade needs to do is attach one end of the tractor with a chain, lie down on the ground and attach the other end of the chain around the ankles. Then only using "hamstring curling leverage muscle power" the tractor is pulled out of the mud. You may omit the tractor pull Comrade but do not skip this exercise.

1. Lying down on the hamstring curl machine, set the pad comfortably a few inches above the heels.

2. Grab on to the handles in the front. As you exhale curl-lift the weight up.

3. Pause at the top, touch the behind (Gluteus Maximus) with the pad and squeeze the hamstrings.

4. As you Inhale slowly bring the weight back down.

#1

STARTING POSITION

HAMSTRING CURLS

#2

PAUSE AT THE TOP AND CONTRACT THE HAMSTRINGS

Straight Leg Deadlifts
This glorious exercise shall make the butt and hamstrings burn. If the Comrade wants to build some (fine looking) legs, this is a key exercise for precisely doing just that. When performing the straight leg deadlifts, keep in mind that it's remarkably similar to the standard deadlift. The main difference is that in the standard deadlift, the legs are bent. In the straight leg deadlifts the legs are always locked out and positioned close together.
(Note) It's recommended doing this exercise on a platform to increase the range of motion. The increased range of motion allows a comrade go through a deeper stretch.

1. Do not start with a heavy weight.

2. Standing in front of the weight with legs together, the Comrade should grip the bar at shoulder width apart and keep both hands turned away from the body (Knuckles pointing away from the body).

3. Keeping the legs locked out. Do not round the back and inhale as the weight is brought down with control.

4. Looking slightly forward is an option.

5. Pause at the bottom and feel a deep stretch in the hamstrings.

6. Exhale as you come up slowly with control.

7. Pause at the top when coming to a fully upright position and tighten the glorious behind (Gluteus Maximus).

#1

STAND ON A PLATFORM SO THAT YOU CAN LOWER THE WEIGHT THROUGH A DEEPER RANGE OF MOTION

STRAIGHT LEG DEADLIFTS

#2

KEEP THE LEGS LOCKED OUT AND INHALE AS YOU COME DOWN. EXHALE AS YOU COME UP AND SQUEEZE THE BUTT.

Training the calves

(Note) When training the calves, many various approaches are available on the market. In the end, they all come down to three basic angle movements.

(Note) In particular, the ladies who excessively walk on high heels for a prolonged period of time run into a problem of tight calves that need serious stretching attention.

(Note) When training the calves, a simple elevated metal platform works great.

1.   Be sure to maintain balance when stepping on the platform. Place only the front third of the shoe soles on the platform.

2.   Slowly come down as far as possible and feel a deep stretch in both calves.

3.   Slowly come up, flex at the top and pause.

The 3 significant positional variations for placing the toes on the platform

• Toes pointing forward (this concentrates calve muscle stimulation down the middle)

• Toes pointing inward (this concentrates calve muscle stimulation on the outside)

• Toes pointing outward (this concentrates calve muscle stimulation on the inside)

COME DOWN AND PAUSE AT THE BOTTOM.

DO NOT JUST GO THROUGH THE MOTION. STRETCH THE CALVES AT THE BOTTOM AND CONTRACT THEM AT THE TOP.

CALVES

COME UP AND CONTRACT THE CALVES AT THE TOP. HOLD THE POSITION FOR A SPLIT SECOND BEFORE GOING BACK DOWN FOR THE STRETCH.

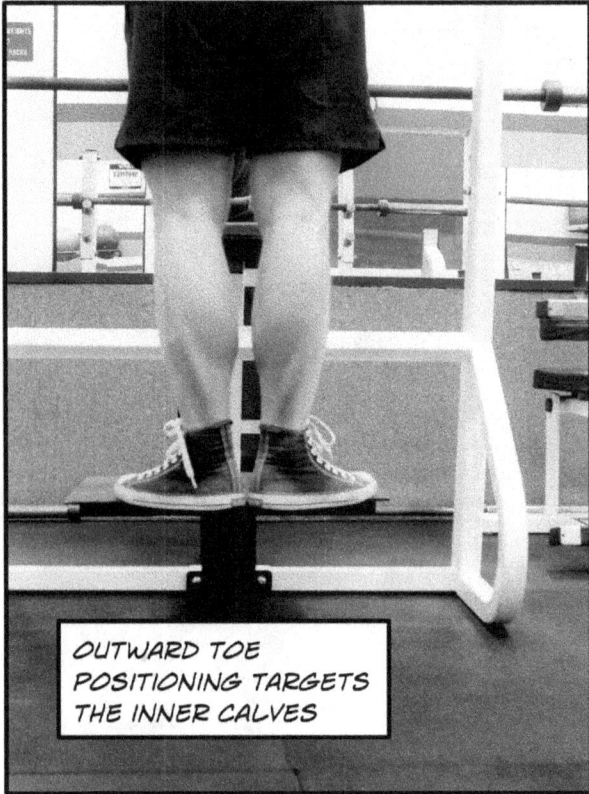

OUTWARD TOE POSITIONING TARGETS THE INNER CALVES

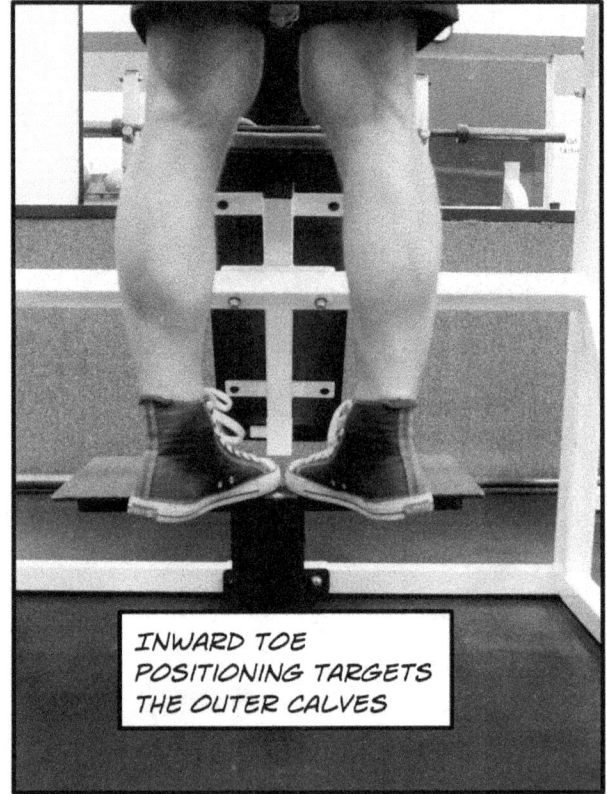

INWARD TOE POSITIONING TARGETS THE OUTER CALVES

STANDARD STARTING POSITION

What is the difference between Comrades who take working out seriously and Comrades who do not? The answer is leg training. Observing individuals in the gym for many years, I can comfortably say that Comrades who train legs go further and excel in the long run because they have the heart to train hard. Leg training is hard training. In Soviet Russia Comrades who skip out on leg training are classified as weekend warriors.

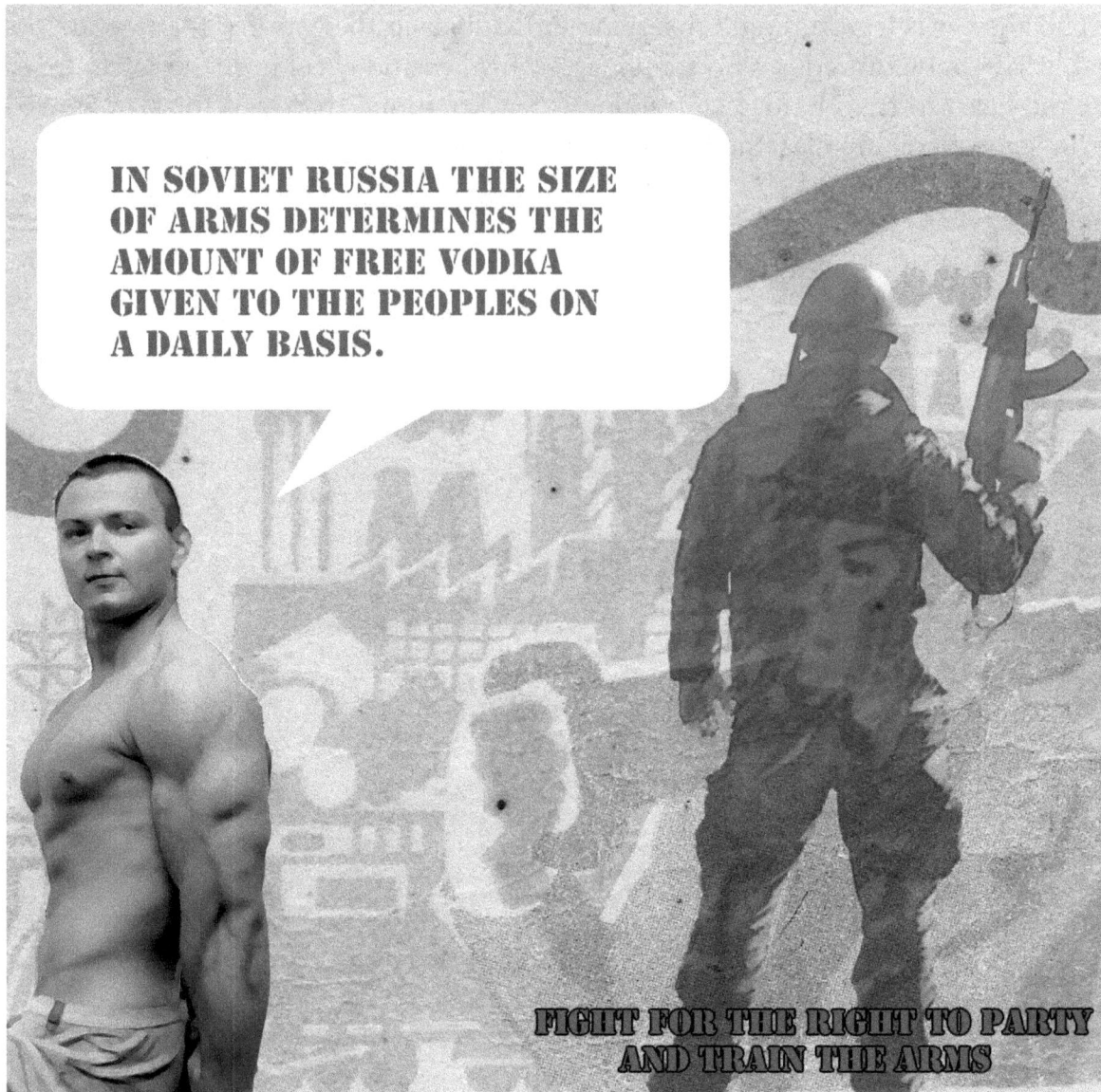

Chapter 12 - Mighty Arms

Glorious arms receive the most favoritism in the gym next to abdominals. Sculpted arms are recognized from a far distance, and they say "A, A, I work out!" Utilize this chapter with enjoyment, keep growing, defining and sculpting those arms. URA!

Notes from the underground
• Arms are perhaps the most trained body part, but it doesn't mean that all Comrades train arms properly. As a matter of fact, if all Comrades applied proper technique and utilized full range of motion they would be light years ahead.
• It seems that the classic bicep curl is the most, over performed exercise of all time. It's a terrific exercise but for the love of everything that is holy Comrades please do something else once in a while. It's ridiculous to see ten Comrades standing in front of the mirror curling dumbbells. This is called the "WTF" moment.

• Please Comrades, remember that triceps need just as much attention as the biceps. (It's not 80/20 split. 80% biceps / 20% triceps) Balance it to 50/50%.

Standing Dumbbell Hammer Curls

In Soviet Russia we call this exercise "The Bear Smash Power Punch" because that's how bears punch out the Spartans who get lost on Russian territory.

(Note) This exercise is executed exceptionally strictly with light to moderate weight.

1. Stand straight with legs at shoulder width apart and slightly bent. Hold two dumbbells of equal weight down on the sides with the heads of the dumbbells pointing forward.

2. Lift the shoulders up and then push them slightly back.

3. As you exhale lift the dumbbells up to a 90 degree angle and pause at the top for a moment. **(Note)** When lifting the dumbbells, the only significant movement that happens is the bending at the elbow. Do not swing the body or throw the shoulders up to aid in the curl.

4. As you inhale slowly lower the dumbbells back down to the starting position.

STARTING POSITION

PAUSE AT THE TOP AND CONTRACT THE BICEPS AS HARD AS POSSIBLE. DO NOT RUSH THE EXERCISE.

EXHALE AS YOU CURL THE DUMBBELLS UP AND INHALE AS YOU BRING THEM DOWN

STANDING DUMBBELL HAMMER CURLS

Behind the Head E-Z Barbell Preacher Curls

This Soviet Russian top secret curling exercise is considered to be highly unorthodox by the outsiders. The range of motion on this bad boy is by far not ordinary.

(Note) If breathing is not timed properly, the Comrade will experience discomfort when performing this exercise.

(Note) Start with lightweight

1. Find a seated or a standing preacher bench. If possible, try to use the backside of the bench. A 90 degree angle located on the backside of the bench isolates the biceps better and allows the muscle belly to go through a deeper contraction.

2. Choose a comfortable weight to start out with. Grab the E-Z curl bar at shoulder width apart.

3. Curl the weight up half way and firmly place the arms on the bench with the under arm area (arm pits) firmly locked over the bench.

4. Lower the weight on the first repetition and allow a few seconds to pass. Stretch the biceps.

5. While exhaling lift the bar up.

6. As the bar comes toward the forehead begin to squeeze the biceps, safely lower the chin and take the bar over the head. (Warning) Practice with a very light weight first. Go slow and unless you are confident about the execution, do not do this exercise without a competent spotter.

7. Pause at the top and keep squeezing the biceps.

8. Slowly inhale and lower the barbell down.

9. You can lift the head after the bar passes back over or keep it down for the remainder of the set (Optional).

10. Bring the bar all the way down. Pause and feel a deep stretch in the biceps.

STARTING POSITION

#1

FULL RANGE OF MOTION COMRADE! DO NOT CHEAT!

KEEP THE ARMS AT FULL EXTENSION BEFORE STARTING THE EXERCISE

BEHIND THE HEAD E-Z BARBELL PREACHER CURLS

#2

AS YOU EXHALE AND BRING THE WEIGHT UP, START TO LOWER THE HEAD TOWARDS THE BENCH AND LOOK DOWN

#3

PAUSE AT THE TOP, CONTRACT THE BICEPS AND BEGIN TO LOWER THE WEIGHT BACK DOWN TO FULL ARM EXTENSION. AS YOU LOWER THE WEIGHT, SLOWLY INHALE.

Reverse E-Z Barbell Curls
Build those forearms and blast the biceps with the reverse E-Z barbell curls.
(Note) Some Comrades have weak wrists and may need to start with lightweight to prevent injury to the wrists.
(Note) This is a great exercise for fighters.
In Soviet Russia this exercise is called "The AK Death Grip". If a Comrade is ever to fall in battle the enemy will not be able to take away his weapon even in death. The grip power lives on long after the Comrade ceases to function.

1.   Find a seated or a standing preacher bench. If possible, try to use the backside of the bench. A 90 degree angle located on the backside of the bench isolates the biceps better and allows the muscle belly to go through a deeper contraction.

2.   Choose a comfortable weight to start out with and grab the E-Z curl bar towards the inside with a reverse grip.

3.   Bring the weight down and firmly place the arms on the bench with the under arm area (arm pits) firmly locked over the bench.

4. As you slowly exhale lift the bar up.

5.   As the bar comes toward the forehead begin to squeeze the biceps hard and pause at the top about an inch away from the forehead. Slightly touching the forehead with the center of the bar is an option.

6.   As you slowly inhale, lower the bar all the way down pausing for about a second at the bottom.

(Note) If the forearms feel like they are burning on the inside, you are doing this exercise right.

REVERSE E-Z BARBELL CURLS

IF YOU BRING THE BAR UP TO FAST YOU MIGHT HIT YOUR HEAD. SLOW DOWN AS YOU COME UP AND ALWAYS STAY IN CONTROL OF THE WEIGHT.

Tricep Rope Pulldowns

For a stunning inner tricep burn, this exercise certainly does the job and then some.

(Note) On tricep training, this is a good exercise to start out with.

When performing the tricep rope pulldowns, the majority of the movement should be happening at the elbows. I have witnessed Comrades lift heavier than they should have; by doing so, they unintentionally threw the shoulders into the exercise.

(Note) If the Comrade feels that he or she is utilizing the shoulders for this exercise it's a strong indication that the weight is too heavy.

(Note) Be sure to have a few days rest in between chest and arm training days. The triceps are heavily taxed during both days.

1. Set the appropriate starting weight and grab the rope at both ends.

2. Slightly lean forward and bring the elbows in towards the body.

3. As you exhale pull the rope down.

4. At the bottom slightly turn the forearms out and squeeze the triceps.

5. As you slowly inhale come back up to starting position.

#1

STARTING POSITION

TRICEP ROPE PULLDOWNS

#2

BRING THE ROPE DOWN, PAUSE AT THE BOTTOM AND CONTRACT THE TRICEPS.

TURN THE FOREARMS OUT AND CONTRACT THE TRICEPS AGAIN FROM THE NEW ANGLE BEFORE TAKING THE ROPE BACK UP.

Dips

Yes Comrade this is a difficult exercise, but it's an important one.

(Note) Dips become easier to do as the Comrade drops fat weight and builds upper body strength.

(Note) If the Comrade can't do this exercise he or she should attempt to perform the first half of the dip (the descending motion), but only if the Comrade is strong enough to do so.

Depending on the variation of dip performed, chest muscles may also be activated.

(Note) To primarily focus on the triceps and not the chest, it's crucial not to lean in forward with the chest or the head. The standard 90 degree angle bend at the elbow focuses primarily on the triceps. Anything below a 90 degree angle bend at the elbow engages the chest as well.

1. Grab hold of the side bars and shift the body weight on to the arms.
(Note) Comrades sometimes rush through dips. Rushing through is not safe. Dips should be done slowly with full control.

2. On the descending motion, inhale and keep the legs bent. Try to stop the downward momentum before heavily activating the chest.
(Note) Dipping down past a 90 degree elbow bend will heavily activate the chest.

3.   Pause at the bottom.

4. As you come back up be sure to exhale. Contract the triceps at the top.

#1

STARTING POSITION

DIPS

#2

STOP AT ABOUT A 90 DEGREE ELBOW ANGLE AND DO NOT LEAN FORWARD TO KEEP THE FOCUS ON THE TRICEPS.

IF YOU LEAN IN TO THE DIP AND GO PAST THE 90 DEGREE ELBOW ANGLE THE FOCUS IS SHIFTED FROM THE TRICEPS TO THE CHEST.

Standing Rear Tricep Presses

In Soviet Russia this exercise is called "The Ivan Press". It's a hugely popular exercise, and everyone whose name is Ivan by default must perform this exercise with perfection one hundred times a day. This is why Ivan The Terrible was always so pissed off. If your name is Ivan and you don't have glorious triceps it's time for you to join the party pal.

1.   Stand up straight and grab hold of the E-Z curl bar.

2.   Grab the bar on the inside with a (close reverse) grip and carefully lift the bar up over the head.

3.   As you inhale slowly lower the weight behind the head keeping the elbows pointing forward or just slightly angled out.

4.   Pause at the bottom and experience a magnificent stretch.

5.   Exhale as you lift the bar back up.

6.   Squeeze the triceps at the top and pause for a split second.

SET UP STEP 1)
HOLD THE BAR WITH A
REVERSE GRIP.

STANDING REAR TRICEP PRESSES

SET UP STEP 2)
LIFT THE BAR TO
SHOULDER HEIGHT.

EXHALE WHEN YOU LIFT THE BAR UP.

#1

INHALE AS YOU BRING THE BAR DOWN AND PAUSE AT THE BOTTOM.

#2

A Spartan walks into a Soviet Russian bar with shield and spear in hand. In Soviet Russia there are no spears or shields. There are only fully automatic glorious dependable arms. The Spartan was never seen again…

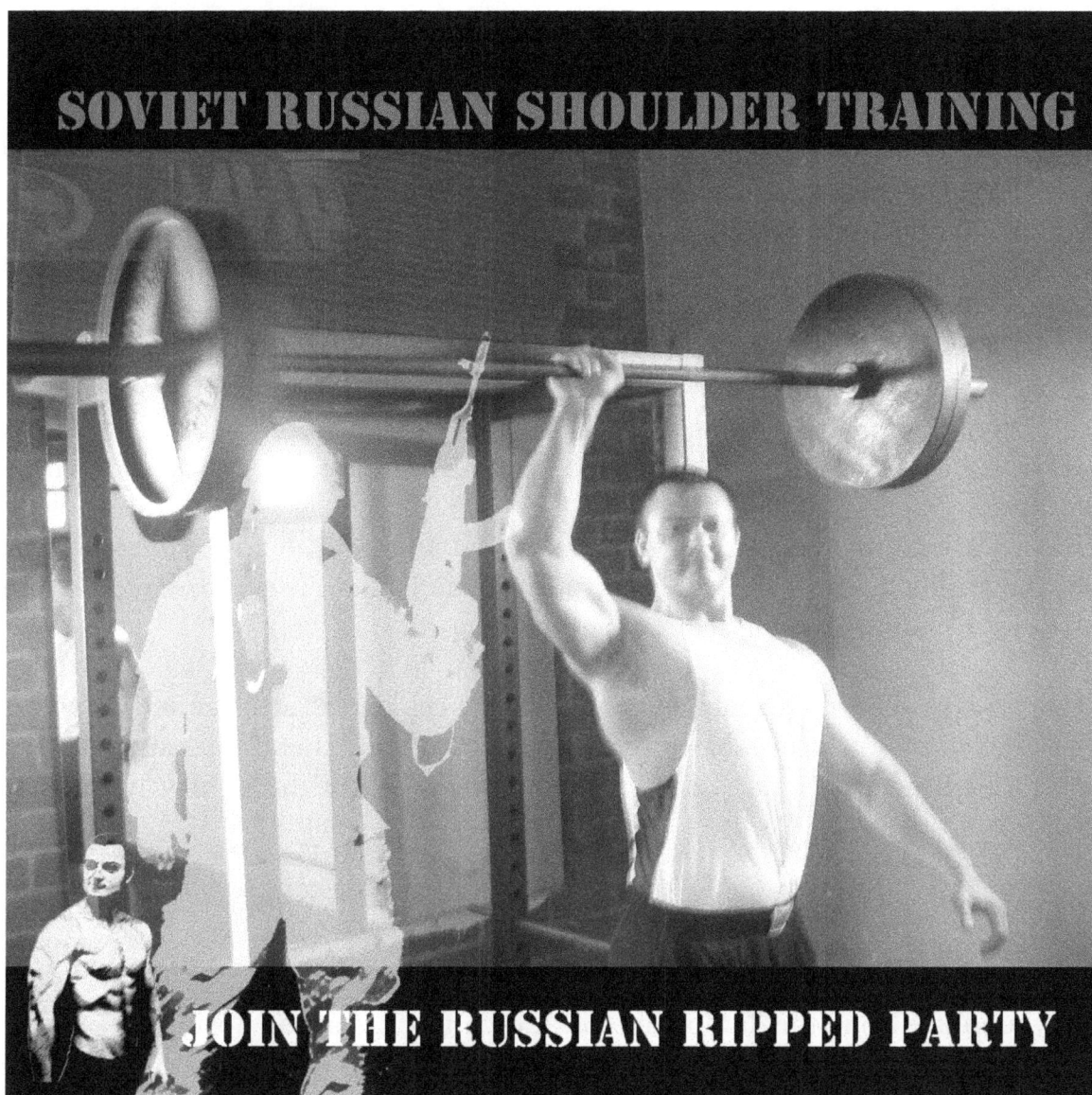

Chapter 13 - Mighty Shoulders

Comrade! Did you know that by losing some fat weight off the body and building quality shoulders you can create an illusion of a respectable looking figure? Round muscular shoulders have a tendency to make a Comrade look slimmer than what he or she actually is. "It's an old Soviet trick."

(Note) I am not saying that shoulders should receive priority training over other body parts. I am however implying that a little extra attention on the shoulders has its benefits in the long run.

Notes from the underground

• Because shoulder joints are excessively used, it's essential for longevity reasons not to jerk any weights (especially) when training the shoulders directly.

• Comrades with bad shoulders should look to resistance band exercises prior to engaging in any free weight shoulder training exercises.

• When training shoulders, do not let the ego push you to lift unusually heavy weights. If a shoulder injury happens because of negligence or ego, it will be your fault and shoulder injuries take a long time to heal. Not worth it.

Lateral Raises

The major purpose of this exercise is to develop the middle portion of the deltoid (shoulder). This is perhaps one of the most fundamental key exercises for shoulder development.

1.   Start by taking two dumbbells of equal weight and hold them on the sides 1-2 inches away from the thighs. **(Note)** Another variation of the lateral raise is to have the dumbbells placed in front of the thighs while slightly leaning forward.

2.   Exhale as you lift the dumbbells to the sides keeping the arms extended with minimal bending at the elbows. **(Note)** Many Comrades cheat and bend the arms at the elbow extensively to lift heavier weight. (Excessive elbow bend is not the right way to perform the lateral raise).

3.   When the arms are parallel or close to parallel with the ground the Comrade should not lift any higher.

4.   As you inhale bring the dumbbells back down to the starting position.

STARTING POSITION
VARIATION 1

#1 LATERAL RAISES

STARTING POSITION
VARIATION 2

Rear Lateral Raise
The major porpoise of this exercise is to build the rear deltoid (shoulder).
(Note) Some Comrades are entirely unaware of the fact that the rear deltoid (shoulder) exists and that it too needs attention.

1.   Select two light dumbbells of equal weight to start.

2.   Lean forward, bend the knees, do not round the back, slightly look up and turn the dumbbells toward each other keeping the arms extended down.

3.   Exhale as you lift the dumbbells up. Try to keep the arms extended as far as possible minimizing the bending at the elbows. **(Note)** It's normal for some elbow bending to occur on this exercise.

4. As you Inhale slowly come back down with control.

STARTING POSITION

#1

REAR LATERAL RAISE

#2

Seated Dumbbell Press

The purpose of this exercise is to focus on the front deltoid (shoulder). In Soviet mother Russia we call this exercise the "I Will Not Give Up Press".

If the enemy ever catches a Comrade and says (hande-ho!) in translation meaning hands up, the Comrade will not be able to comply since no dumbbells are available in each hand. Surrender is not an option.

1.   The Comrade is to sit on a bench that has a backrest and select comfortable starting weight.

2.   Lift the dumbbells up by placing them on the knees and kick them up one at a time; just as the Comrade would do for the (incline dumbbell press).

3.   Turn the dumbbells out, keeping the arms at or close to parallel level with the ground.

4.   Exhale and press up with control. When the dumbbells make contact overhead stop for a split second.

5. As you Inhale lower the dumbbells back down to the starting parallel position. **(Note)** Some Comrades go below parallel for a deeper stretch. If this option is chosen, it's to be executed with caution and slow speed.

STANDARD STARTING
POSITION

#1 SEATED DUMBBELL PRESS

DEEP STARTING
POSITION

EXHALE AS YOU LIFT
THE DUMBBELLS UP

Dumbbell shrugs

Dumbbell Shrugs are classified as a back exercise that primarily focuses on the trapezius. **(Note)** In Soviet Russia performing this particular exercise with shoulder training is standard practice. As a matter of fact, the "Dumbell Shrugs" are also known "Shoulder Shrugs."

1.   The Comrade is to grab two moderate-weight dumbbells of equal weight and hold them on the sides of the thighs.

2. As you exhale shrug the dumbbells up. When sliding the dumbbells on the sides of the body, the arms should not assist in the lift. **(Note)** On heavy shrugs, wrist straps may be utilized as an aid.

3.   Pause at the top and squeeze the muscles. **(Note)** The Comrade should attempt to touch the earlobes with the shoulders.

4. As you slowly inhale lower the dumbbells back down.

5.   Stretch at the bottom. **(Note)** The Comrade can also do this exercise while holding the dumbbells in front of the thighs.

DUMBBELL SHRUGS

E-Z Barbell Upright Rows

This exercise focuses on the front deltoid, (shoulder) and it stretches the trapezius too. This exercise can be performed with a straight bar or an E-Z curl bar. **(Note)** It's important to try and keep the body straight while performing the exercise without excessive rocking.

1.   With a reverse grip, grab the bar towards the inside.

2.   As you exhale, lift the bar up leading with the elbows. **(Note)** Some Comrades lift the bar to the neck while others stop around the upper chest level. Try both versions.

3.   As you inhale, lower the bar down.

#1

STARTING POSITION

E-Z BARBELL UPRIGHT ROWS

#2

LIFT VARIATION 1. LIFT THE BAR TOWARDS THE UPPER CHEST AREA.

#2-B

LIFT VARIATION NUMBER 2. LIFT THE BAR TO THE CLAVICLE BONE LEVEL.

If a Comrade wishes to get fancy with other shoulder exercises it's entirely ok to do so. The exercises presented in this chapter are what you call the meat and potatoes and borsh of shoulder training. If the Comrade chooses only to do the shoulder exercises presented in this chapter, he or she will be able to build glorious shoulders.

RUSSIA (1975) THE YEAR ALL PEOPLE WERE FORBIDDEN TO WEAR SHIRTS

ABDOMINAL TRAINING

Chapter 14 - Awesomeness Glorious Abbs

Every Comrade has glorious abbs hidden underneath the protective layer. However, only a small percentage of Comrades actually have the abdominals visible.

So how does a Comrade get his or her abbs out?

The Russian Ripped way to get the abdominals out from underneath the fat, is by eating a clean diet, doing lots of cardio and maintaining a sound resistance training program.

(Note) Based on the Soviet Russian Institute for Glorious Abb Power: To get the abdominals out in the sun, it's (70% diet, 20% cardiovascular activity, 8% resistance training and only 2% direct abdominal training).

Ilya Sulima

Notes from the underground
- If a Comrade trains the abdominals heavily for a long period of time, the abdominals will grow. **(Note)** When the fat comes off the abdominals, prior heavy training will most likely make the abbs bulky looking with deep cuts and separation.
- If a Comrade wants model like non accented slim abbs, abdominal training should not exceed one session per week to prevent abdominal growth.

Straight Hanging Leg Lifts
In Soviet Russia, this is the most popular abdominal exercise of all time. It's so popular that even bears do it. This exercise targets the lower, middle and upper abdomen regions. It provides an excellent over all stretch. If a Comrade has difficulties at first, he or she should start with a few repetitions and work up from there.

(Note) If the Comrade cannot perform any repetitions, he or she should attempt to hold the legs out in a partial extended position for as long as possible.

1. Grab on to a pullup bar with a wide grip keeping the legs together and straight.

2. As you exhale, slowly lift the legs up straight without bending to a 90 degree angle or higher. **(Note)** Do not rush and try to pause for a moment when the legs are roughly parallel to the ground.

3. As you inhale, slowly lower the legs back down

216

#1

STARTING POSITION

STRAIGHT HANGING LEG LIFTS

#2

EXHALE AS YOU LIFT THE LEGS UP

Seated Bench Leg Lift Crunches

On this exercise, the lower the Comrade goes towards a parallel full body extension, the more strain he or she puts on the abdominals. This exercise focuses primarily on the upper and middle section of the abdominals.

(Note) When the body is in the fully extended position balanced on the bench, going below parallel to the ground is not suggested.

1. The Comrade is to sit down on a bench and grab the bench toward the front. **(Note)** Holding on to the bench helps with balance. Even if the Comrade has superb balance, it's still recommended that he or she hold on to the bench.

2. As you exhale, flex the abdominals and bring the knees towards the chest.

3. Pause for a split second at the top.

4. Inhale as you come back to the starting extended position.

#1

STARTING POSITION

SEATED BENCH LEG LIFT CRUNCHES

#2

Cable Pulldowns

In Soviet Russia, the cable pulldown exercise is usually incorporated with other abdominal exercises. This exercise mainly focuses on the top and middle section of the abdominals.

1. The Comrade is to find a comfortable bar and floor padding. **(Note)** The cable pulldowns can be done from a standing or kneeling position.

2. Set the appropriate weight.

3. Grab hold of the bar and use the body weight to assist in slowly bringing down the weight to the starting position. **(Note)** Keep distance from the moving weight. No Comrade wants to accidentally hit his or her head on any moving metal.

4. As you exhale take the weight down while holding the bar with the arms bent behind the head. **(Note)** If possible, slightly touch the thighs with the elbows.

5. Inhale as you come back up with control keeping the arms bent.

#1 STARTING POSITION

CABLE PULLDOWNS

#2 ENDING POSITION

I bet some of you thought that it takes Soviet Russian Rocket Science to train abdominals. Well it doesn't. The three basic abdominal exercises presented in this chapter will do the job just fine.

(Note) Everyone starts at a different fitness level. Giving up should never be an option. "Giving up is only an option if the Comrade leaves that option open." For some it will take longer than others to get their abbs out. Achieving fat free glorious abdominals shows that you are serious about training. Weekend warrior training approach is not serious stuff. The majority are weekend warriors. Are you?

The Abdominal Formula

Abdominals = Low Body Fat

Low Body Fat = Clean (Healthy) diet + Resistance training + Cardiovascular training + Time + Patience + Persistence

IN SOVIET RUSSIA CARDIO DO YOU

Chapter 15 – Run Comrade Run!
The Cardio Fat Blast

Cardiovascular training Comrade is something that Comrades run away from without physically running. I have seen Comrades entirely avoid cardiovascular training or pretend like they can do cardio for ten minutes and then call it quits.

Bad choice!

Why?

Well, it takes the body on average of 10-15 minutes to enter the fat burning zone. So please, for the love of everything that is holy, don't do cardiovascular training for less than 20-30 minutes at a time unless health issues exist that prevent you from doing so.

(Note) If a Comrade wants to burn the fat, a moderate difficulty, long cardio session should be regularly implemented.

(Note) It's important for Comrades who are just coming around to training from a sedentary lifestyle not to push themselves to a point of burn out. A slow, consistent plan of cardio progression is outlined in this chapter just for that specific reason.

(Note) Cardiovascular aka fat burning training is to be performed after resistance training, not before.

(Note) When selecting a starting point for cardio, be honest with yourself. Keep in mind that every two weeks the difficulty level increases.

The Multi Stage Cardio Training Program is designed to be implemented over a period of time. Why? Because taking off the fat takes time. Some fitness "professionals" may disagree with the long term strategy and present a two or three month quick fix plan. Many of those "professionals" only focus on the average and the already fit Comrades. The tree month plan is insufficient time to get in shape for everyone. The Russian Ripped philosophy strives for all Comrades to have a starting reference cardio point regardless of the fitness level. As already mentioned, taking off fat takes time. However, if the cardio program is implemented properly, in the long run the fat comes off and stays off. So keep a positive can do attitude and step in to a better looking you one week at a time.

Stage One Cardio

For all those Comrades who have bad joints or who are just getting into the cardiovascular theater, it's suggested they start out with the stationary bike. (If health permits) The stationary bike is easy on the joints and not as rigorous as other cardio machines.

A) 20 minutes 3 days a week for 2 weeks.
B) 20 minutes 5 days a week for 2 weeks.
C) 30 minutes 3 days a week for 2 weeks.
D) 30 minutes 5 days a week for 2 weeks.
E) 45 minutes 3 days a week for 2 weeks.
F) 45 minutes 5 days a week for 2 weeks.
G) 60 minutes 3 days a week for 2 weeks.
H) 60 minutes 5 days a week for 2 weeks.

(Graduate to Stage Two) If no joint problems or other health problems are preventing you from doing so.

Stage Two Cardio
Treadmill

The majority of Comrades should strive to start at this cardio stage or beyond. Most treadmills have the option of setting the speed and the incline level. **(Note)** Please take the time to locate the emergency stop button on the treadmill.

(Note) When stopping the treadmill, it does not stop right away. Keep walking after you pressed the stop button and do not stop walking until the treadmill comes to a complete stop on its own.

A) 20 minutes 3 days a week for 2 weeks. (no incline) speed/ 3.0mph
B) 20 minutes 5 days a week for 2 weeks. (level 1 incline) speed/ 3.0mph
C) 30 minutes 3 days a week for 2 weeks. (level 2 incline) speed/ 3.5mph
D) 30 minutes 5 days a week for 2 weeks. (level 3 incline) speed/ 3.5mph
E) 45 minutes 3 days a week for 2 weeks. (level 4 incline) speed/ 4.0mph
F) 45 minutes 5 days a week for 2 weeks. (level 5 incline) speed/ 4.0mph
G) 60 minutes 3 days a week for 2 weeks. (level 6 incline) speed/ 4.5mph
H) 60 minutes 5 days a week for 2 weeks (level 7 incline) speed/ 4.5mph
(Graduate to Stage Three)

Stage Three Cardio
Running

Yes many Comrades hate running. But Comrades who commit to running for only a few months typically have a complete change of opinion on the matter. Running is a glorious fat annihilator that hurts in the beginning but pays off amazingly in the end. There was once a time I hated to run. After the six pack came out I realized how wrong it was of me to hate such an amazing thing. Running is an effective approach that is guaranteed to work. Don't cut yourself short. Fight, huff and puff through the pain in the beginning. After all you want to get ripped right?

(Note) Having proper running shoes and staying consistent through the first few runs is critical. With every pound dropped the running becomes easier.

A)2 miles 3 times a week for 2 weeks
B)2 miles 4 times a week for 2 weeks
C)2 miles 5 times a week for 2 weeks
D)3 miles 3 times a week for 2 weeks
E) 3 miles 4 times a week for 2 weeks
F) 3 miles 5 times a week for 2 weeks
G)5 miles 3 times a week for 2 weeks
H) 5 miles 4 times a week for 2 weeks
I) 6 miles 4 times a week for 2 weeks
(Graduate to Stage Four)

Stage Four Cardio
Stairmaster the Fat Blaster

There are two common variations of the Stairmaster. The first variation is a conveyor belt type. As the Comrade steps up, the stairs roll down. The second type of Stairmaster is a machine that has two separate pedal steppers that move downward as the Comrade shifts the body weight on each pedal independently.

(Note) If you lean on the railing you are cheating. The rails are for the Comrade to lightly grip and maintain balance only.

A) 30 minutes 3 times a week for 2 weeks / level 5
B) 30 minutes 5 times a week for 2 weeks / level 5
C) 40 minutes 3 times a week for 2 weeks / level 5
D) 40 minutes 5 times a week for 2 weeks / level 5
E) 50 minutes 5 times a week for 2 weeks / level 5
F) 60 minutes 5 times a week for 2 weeks / level 5
G) 60 minutes 5 times a week for 2 weeks / level 6
H) 70 minutes 5 times a week for 2 weeks / level 3
I) 70 minutes 5 times a week for 2 weeks / level 4
J) 70 minutes 5 times a week for 2 weeks / level 5
(Graduate to Stage Five)

Stage Five

Stage five training is presented in the next chapter.
(Note) Stage five training is immediately followed by stage 2, 3 or 4 cardio routine as presented in this chapter. Stage five training is also known as Combo Training.

Lazy Man Cardio

Do you like to watch new and exciting movies or shows Comrade? I know I do. Sometimes I want to watch a new flick, but due to time constraints it doesn't work out. Enter the greatest cardio invention ever. (Lazy Man Cardio)

(Note) This type of cardio is best done when the Comrade has lots of time.

Here, is what's needed for Lazy Man Cardio

1) Treadmill (Stairmaster works too for the more advanced Comrades)

2) Portable DVD player, or a fancy smart phone, or a smart pad.

3) Headphones

4) A new movie or a favorite flick.

5) Towel

6) Water

The way this works is simple.

1) Hook up the DVD / smart phone to a power source if the battery can't run for long on its own.

2) Set the treadmill on an incline level of (2 - 4) and a speed of (3.0- 3.5 mph).
(Note) If doing Lazy Man Cardio on the Stairmaster: levels 3-6 work great.

3)   Put the towel over the display.

4)   Lightly hold the front or side railing for stability and let the movie play.

5)   Do not get off the treadmill until the tread stops 100 minutes later by default, or continue walking till the movie ends.

This is a glorious fat burning method that keeps the mind away from boredom. When the Comrade immerses him or herself in a good movie, the mind forgets about the time spent on the treadmill or the Stairmaster. When the mind is elsewhere, the body sets itself on autopilot. In Soviet Russia we call this The Fat Burning Autopilot Mode. I don't know why everyone who has problems in the cardio fat burning department isn't applying this method to fight the fat and stay entertained at the same time.

"This is what you call killing two bears with one dumbbell."

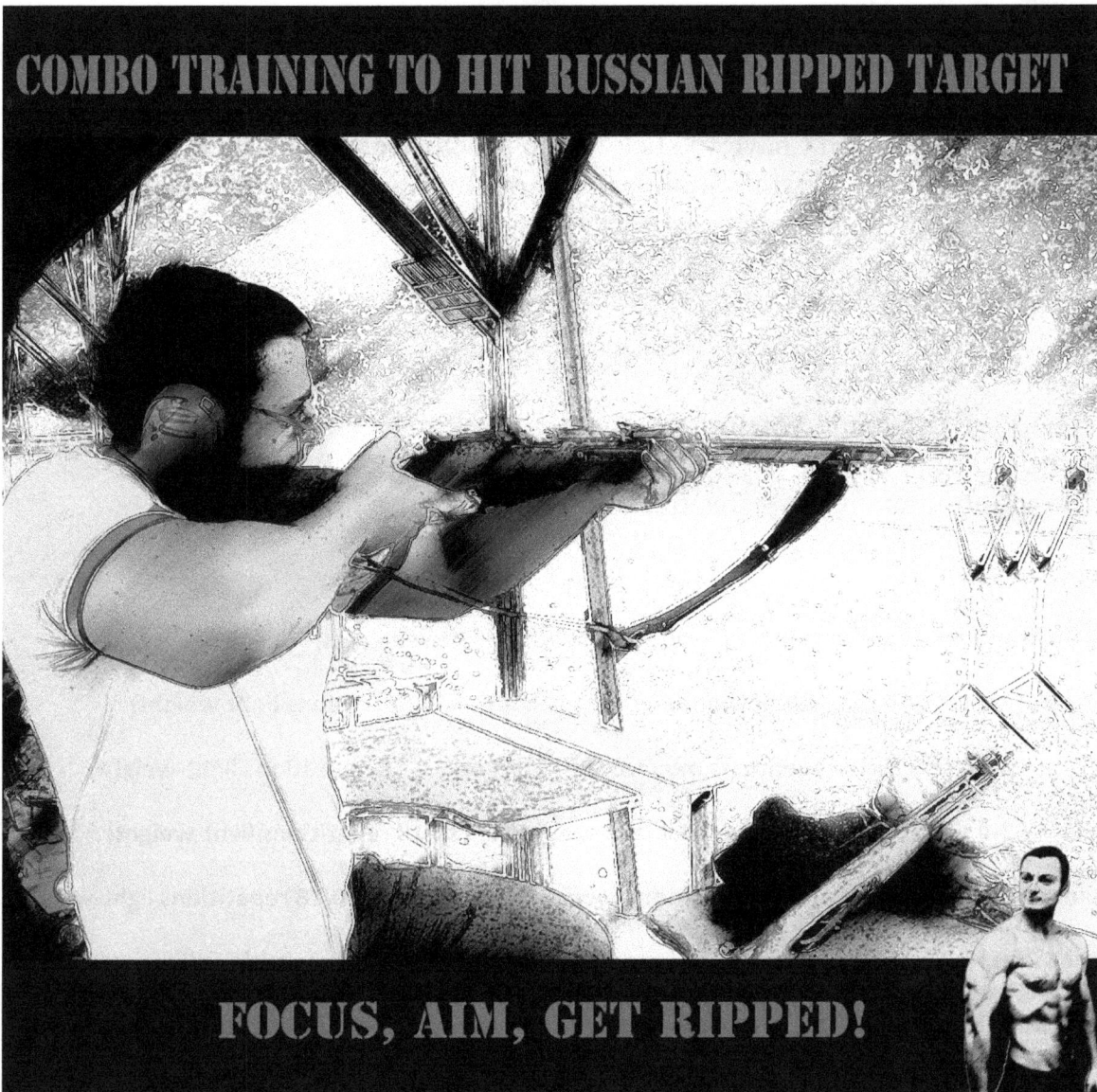

COMBO TRAINING TO HIT RUSSIAN RIPPED TARGET

FOCUS, AIM, GET RIPPED!

Chapter 16 - Combo It Up Comrade!

Ok Comrade, so far we covered some specific approaches on training major muscle groups as well as fat fighting cardio stages. In this chapter, we will apply additional information to the established basic training principals and expand into "Combo Training". Combo Training is the back bone training approach that most Comrades follow to get Russian Ripped. Combo Training is also another name for (stage five) training as noted in the previous chapter. When a Comrade thinks of Combo training, a hybrid bear-wolf animal should be visualized. This bear-wolf animal is notable because he is strong like bear (Resistance training) and lean like wolf (Fat blasting cardio training).

Basic Pre-Combo routine examples
Specific body part training utilizing basic non combo principals

(Note) All though you don't have to stick to the specific schedule examples presented below, you should get a rough idea about how you might want to structure personal workouts combined with a basic stage 1, 2, 3 or 4 cardio session.

The examples below are workouts a Comrade might want to do before getting involved in a full on Russian Ripped Combo training routine.

(Note) Think of pre-combo training as high school and combo training as a university. It makes logical sense to do one before the other.
(Note) Pre-combo training prepares the Comrade for combo training.

(Reference Chapter 9)

<u>Chest Day</u> **(light-moderate weight) (30 sec – 90 sec rest period between sets)**

Bench Press / 3-4 sets (8-10 repetitions moderate-weight) or (10-18 repetitions light-weight)

Dumbbell Press / 3-4 sets (8-10 repetitions moderate-weight) or (10-18 repetitions light-weight)

Dumbbell Flys / 3-4 sets (8-10 repetitions moderate-weight) or (10-18 repetitions light-weight)

Incline Dumbbell Press / 3-4 sets (8-10 repetitions moderate-weight) or (10-18 repetitions light-weight)

Incline Bench Press / 3-4 sets (8-10 repetitions moderate-weight) or (10-18 repetitions light-weight)

Incline Dumbbell Flys / 3-4 sets (8-10 repetitions moderate-weight) or (10-18 repetitions light-weight)

Decline Dumbbell Press / 3-4 sets (8-10 repetitions moderate-weight) or (10-18 repetitions light-weight)

Decline Bench Press / 3-4 sets (8-10 repetitions moderate-weight) or (10-18 repetitions ligh- weight)

At the end add a basic stage 1, 2, 3 or 4 cardio session

(Reference Chapter 10)

<u>Back Day</u> **(light-moderate weight) (30 sec – 90 sec rest period between sets)**

Wide Grip Lat Pulldowns / 3-4 sets (8-10 repetitions moderate-weight) or (10-18 repetitions light-weight)

Wide Grip Pullups / 3 sets (6-10 repetitions)

Close Grip Lat Pulldowns (V handle) / 3-4 sets (8-10 repetitions moderate- weight) or (10-18 repetitions light-weight)

Close Grip Chinups / 3 sets (6-10 repetitions)

T- Bar Row / 3-4 sets (8-10 repetitions moderate-weight) or (10-18 repetitions light-weight)

Wide Grip Cable Rows / 3-4 sets (8-10 repetitions moderate-weight) or (10-18 repetitions light-weight)

The Dead Lift / 3-4 sets (8-10 repetitions moderate-weight) or (10-18 repetitions light-weight)

Lower Back Extensions / 3-4 sets (8-10 repetitions)

At the end add a basic stage 1, 2, 3 or 4 cardio session

(Reference Chapter 11)

Leg Day *(light-moderate weight) (30 sec – 90 sec rest period between sets)*

Soviet Squat / 3-4 sets (8-10 repetitions moderate-weight) or (10-18 repetitions light-weight)

Dumbbell Duck Squat / 3-4 sets (8-10 repetitions moderate-weight) or (10-18 repetitions light-weight)

Leg Extensions / 3-4 sets (8-10 repetitions moderate-weight) or (10-18 repetitions light-weight)

Hamstring Curls / 3-4 sets (8-10 repetitions moderate-weight) or (10-18 repetitions light-weight)

Straight Leg Deadlifts / 3-4 sets (8-10 repetitions moderate-weight) or (10-18 repetitions light-weight)

At the end add a basic stage 1, 2, 3 or 4 cardio session

(Reference Chapter 12)

Arm Day *(light-moderate weight) (30 sec – 90 sec rest period between sets)*

Standing Dumbbell Hammer Curls / 3-4 sets (8-10 repetitions moderate- weight) or (10-18 repetitions light-weight)

Behind the Head E-Z Barbell Preacher Curls/ 3-4 sets (8-10 repetitions moderate-weight) or (10-18 repetitions light-weight)

Reverse E-Z Barbell Curls/ 3-4 sets (8-10 repetitions moderate-weight) or (10-18 repetitions light-weight)

Tricep Cable Rope Pulldowns / 3-4 sets (8-10 repetitions moderate-weight) or (10-18 repetitions light-weight)

Dips / 3-4 sets (8-10 repetitions moderate-weight)

Standing Rear Tricep Presses / 3-4 sets (8-10 repetitions moderate-weight) or (10-18 repetitions light-weight)

At the end add a basic stage 1, 2, 3 or 4 cardio session

(Reference Chapter 13)

<u>Shoulder Day</u> (light-moderate weight) (30 sec – 90 sec rest period between sets)

Lateral Raises / 3-4 sets (8-10 repetitions moderate-weight) or (10-18 repetitions light-weight)

Rear Lateral Raise / 3-4 sets (8-10 repetitions moderate-weight) or (10-18 repetitions light-weight)

Seated Dumbbell Press / 3-4 sets (8-10 repetitions moderate-weight) or (10-18 repetitions light-weight)

Dumbbell shrugs / 3-4 sets (8-10 repetitions moderate-weight) or (10-18 repetitions light-weight)

E-Z Barbell upright Rows / 3-4 sets (8-10 repetitions moderate-weight) or (10-18 repetitions light-weight)

At the end add a basic stage 1, 2, 3 or 4 cardio session

(Reference Chapters 11 and 14)

<u>Abdominals and Calves Day</u> (light-moderate weight)(<u>>30 sec</u> rest period between sets)

Straight Hanging Leg Lifts 10-20 repetitions / 3-4 sets

Seated Bench Leg Lift Crunches 10-20 repetitions / 3-4 sets

Cable Pulldowns 10-20 repetitions / 3sets

Calves variation-1 10-20 repetitions / 3 sets

Calves variation-2 10-20 repetitions / 3 sets

Calves variation-3 10-20 repetitions / 3 sets

At the end add a basic stage 1, 2, 3 or 4 cardio session

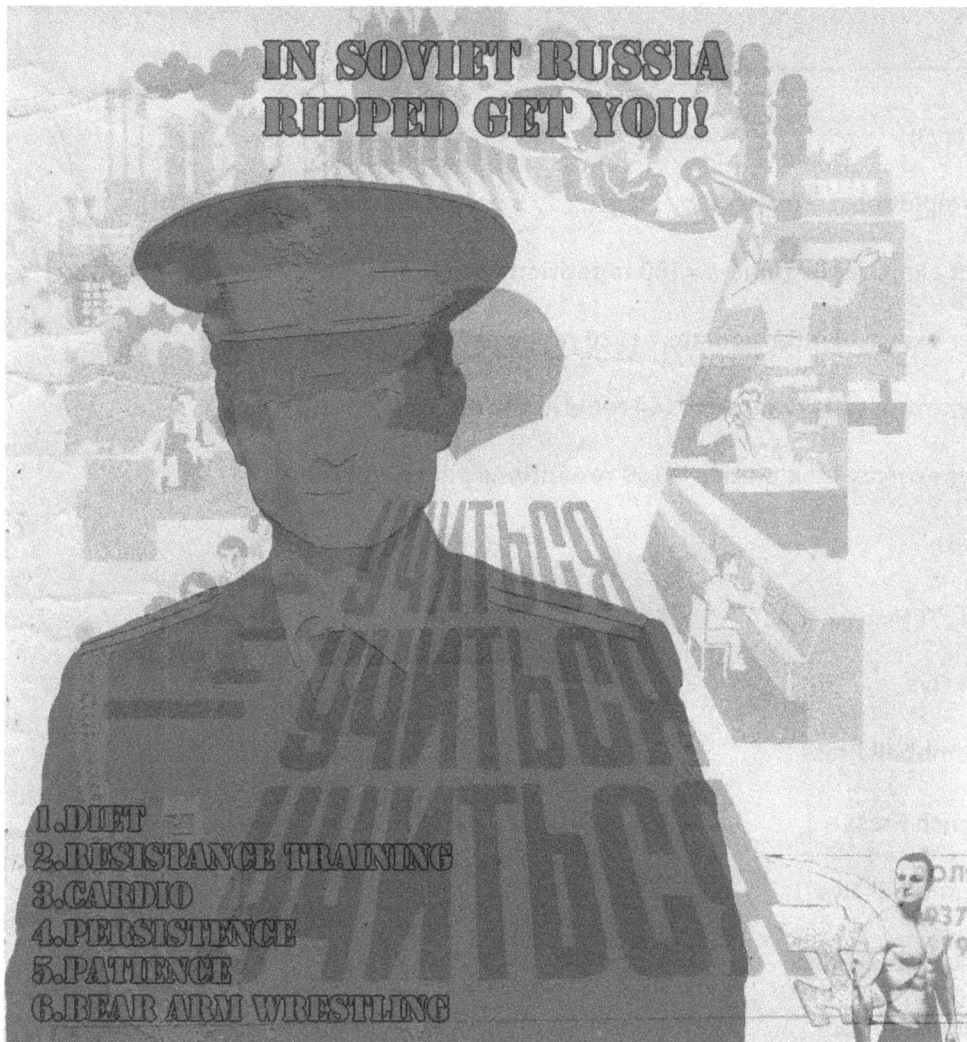

Combo Training / Stage Five Training

Combo Training is a combination of exercises from specific (body part / training days). Each combination counts for one completion. Multiple completions can add up to (100 to 600 +) repetitions per workout.

(Note) The first goal is to accomplish more completions than in the previous session. The second goal is to use more weight. While performing the circuit, the rest time is almost nonexistent between exercises.

(Note) Moving from one exercise to another at a fast pace is the rest time.

The Comrade must complete one exercise and rapidly move on to the next. The rest period should become shorter and shorter between completions as training progresses over time.

(Note) It's not recommended to do combo training aka (Stage Five Training) during peak gym hours.

(Reference Chapter 9)

Chest Day (2-6 Completions) (*Followed by stage 1, 2, 3 or 4 cardio session*)

(10 repetitions per exercise) beginners = (80 repetitions per completion)

(15 repetitions per exercise) intermediate = (120 repetitions per completion)

(18 repetitions per exercise) advanced= (144 repetitions per completion)

(20 repetitions per exercise) the crazies= (160 repetitions per completion)

- **Bench Press**

- **Dumbbell Press**

- **Dumbbell Flys**

- **Incline Dumbbell Press**

- **Incline Bench Press**

- **Incline Dumbbell Flys**

- **Decline Dumbbell Press**

- **Decline Bench Press**

(Reference Chapter 10)

Back Day (2-6 Completions) (*Followed by 1, 2, 3 or 4 stage cardio session*)

(10 repetitions per exercise) beginners = (80 repetitions per completion)

(15 repetitions per exercise) intermediate = (120 repetitions per completion)

(18 repetitions per exercise) advanced= (144 repetitions per completion)

(20 repetitions per exercise) the crazies= (160 repetitions per completion)

- **Wide Grip Lat Pulldowns**

- **Wide Grip Pullups (Maximum number of repetition varies)**

- **Close Grip Lat Pulldowns (V handle)**

- **Close Grip Chinups (Maximum number of repetition varies)**

- **T- Bar Row**

- **Wide Grip Cable Rows**

- **The Dead Lift**

- **Lower Back Extensions**

(Reference Chapter 11)

Leg Day (2-6 Completions) (*Followed by stage 1, 2, 3 or 4 cardio session*)

(12 repetitions per exercise) beginners = (60 repetitions per completion)

(15 repetitions per exercise) intermediate = (75 repetitions per completion)

(18 repetitions per exercise) advanced= (90 repetitions per completion)

(20 repetitions per exercise) the crazies= (100 repetitions per completion)

- **Soviet Squat**

- **Dumb Bell Duck Squat**

- **Leg Extensions**

- **Hamstring Curls**

- **Straight Leg Deadlifts**

(Reference Chapter 12)

Arm Day (2-6 Completions) (*Followed by stage 1, 2, 3 or 4 cardio session*)

 (15 repetitions per exercise) beginners = (90 repetitions per completion)

(18 repetitions per exercise) intermediate = (108 repetitions per completion)

(20 repetitions per exercise) advanced= (120 repetitions per completion)

(25 repetitions per exercise) the crazies= (150 repetitions per completion)

- **Standing Dumbbell Hammer Curls**

- **Behind the Head E-Z Barbell Preacher Curls**

- **Reverse E-Z Barbell Curls**

- **Tricep Cable Rope Pulldowns**

- **Dips**

- **Standing Rear Tricep Presses**

(Reference Chapter 13)

Shoulder Day (2-6 Completions) (*Followed by stage 1, 2, 3 or 4 cardio session*)

(12 repetitions per exercise) beginners = (60 repetitions per completion)

(15 repetitions per exercise) intermediate = (75 repetitions per completion)

(18 repetitions per exercise) advanced= (90 repetitions per completion)

(20 repetitions per exercise) the crazies= (100 repetitions per completion)

- **Lateral Raises**

- **Rear Lateral Raise**

- **Seated Dumbbell Press**

- **Dumb Bell shrugs**

- **E-Z Barbell upright Rows**

(Reference Chapters 11 and 14)

Abdominals and Calves Day

(2-6 Completions) (*Followed by stage 1, 2, 3 or 4 cardio session)*

(15 repetitions per exercise) beginners = (90 repetitions per completion)

(18 repetitions per exercise) intermediate = (108 repetitions per completion)

(20 repetitions per exercise) advanced= (120 repetitions per completion)

(25 repetitions per exercise) the crazies= (150 repetitions per completion)

- **Straight Hanging Leg Lifts**

- **Seated Bench Leg Lift Crunches**

- **Cable Pulldowns**

- **Calves variation-1**

- **Calves variation-2**

- **Calves variation-3**

Any Comrade who can properly stick to combo training for a few months will see amazing results.

(Note) I highly encourage all Comrades to work up to combo training and not immediately jump into it. Russian Ripped training is not a (20 minute a day, 3 times a week training program). It's a program of progression that takes time.
(Note) Start of by going through the cardio stages and pre-combo training routines to build yourself up.

The next chapter presents a comprehensive long term week by week training guideline.

Chapter 17 - The 6 Step Plan to Victory!

Not all Comrades have the time to implement the long term training routine presented in this chapter. This is understandable, and therefore it is recommended that the busy Comrades stick to the basic principles of body part isolation training and cardiovascular stage progression as presented in the previous chapters. But, if you are a lucky Comrade who has the time to implement the following plan, please keep in mind that this plan is not a quick fix solution. This plan is a long term commitment. No gimmicks, no shortcuts and no BS. Take the time to consider if you want to stick with basic training which will provide consistent results, or, if you want to proceed on with the long term structured training plan outlined in this chapter.

(Level 1) Get Focused and Get Moving
Level 1 is directed towards the Comrades who are out of shape or may have other health issues.

The rules of Level 1 training are listed below.

1. If health allows, the Comrade is to follow the cardiovascular stages of progression. **(Note)** Check back with chapter 15 to reference cardiovascular stage progression.

2. If health allows, the Comrade is to try and follow basic resistance training. **(Note)** Check back with chapters 9-14 and start slow.

Healthy Comrades should strive to start training at Level 2 or above.

(Level 2) Fight the Good Fight

Length of level 2 training (12 weeks)

<u>*Abdominals and calves*</u> *are to be incorporated and trained once a week prior to cardiovascular training.*

Week 1

Beginner Combo Training

(10 repetitions per exercise light-weight) 3-5 combos

Concentration is on one major body part per day followed by (*treadmill*) *cardio* training of 30 minutes.

(<u>Treadmill settings</u> / incline level 3 / speed level 3 mph)

Training frequency of week 1: minimum of 5 days

Week 2

Non Combo standard training (8-12 repetitions per set / 3- 4 sets / 4-5 exercises of choice / light-moderate weight)

Concentration is on one major body part per day followed by (*treadmill*) *cardio*

60 minutes. (<u>Treadmill settings</u> / incline level 6 / speed level 2.5 mph)

Training frequency of week 2: minimum of 5 days

Week 3

Beginner Combo Training

(10 repetitions per exercise light-weight) 3-5 combos

Concentration is on one major body part per day followed by (*treadmill*) *cardio* training of 30 minutes.

(<u>Treadmill settings</u> / incline level 4 / speed level 3 mph)

Training frequency of week 3: minimum of 5 days

Week 4

Non Combo standard training (8-12 repetitions per set / 3- 4 sets / 4-5 exercises of choice / light-moderate weight)

Concentration is on one major body part per day followed by (*treadmill) cardio*

60 minutes. (Treadmill settings / incline level 6 / speed level 2.7 mph)

Training frequency of week 4: minimum of 5 days

Week 5

Beginner Combo Training

(10 repetitions per exercise light-weight) 3-5 combos

Concentration is on one major body part per day followed by (*treadmill) cardio* training of 30 minutes.

(Treadmill settings / incline level 4 / speed level 3 mph)

Training frequency of week 5: minimum of 5 days

Week 6

(Treadmill) cardio no weight training

60 minutes. (Treadmill settings / incline level 5 / speed level 3.5 mph)

Training frequency of week 6: minimum of 6 days

Week 7

Non Combo standard training (8-12 repetitions per set / 3- 4 sets / 4-5 exercises of choice / light-moderate weight)

Concentration is on one major body part per day followed by (*treadmill) cardio*

60 minutes. (Treadmill settings / incline level 6 / speed level 3.0 mph)

Training frequency of week 7: minimum of 5 days

Week 8

Beginner Combo Training

(10 repetitions per exercise light-weight) <u>4-5</u> combos

Concentration is on one major body part per day followed by (*treadmill) cardio* training of 35 minutes.

(<u>Treadmill settings</u> / incline level 4 / speed level 3 mph)

Training frequency of week 8: minimum of 5 days

Week 9

Non Combo standard training (8-12 repetitions per set / 3- 4 sets / 4-5 exercises of choice / light-moderate weight)

Concentration is on one major body part per day followed by (*treadmill) cardio*

60 minutes. (<u>Treadmill settings</u> / incline level 6 / speed level 3.5 mph)

Training frequency of week 9: minimum of 5 days

Week 10

Beginner Combo Training

(10 repetitions per exercise light-weight) <u>5</u> combos

Concentration is on one major body part per day followed by (*treadmill) cardio* training of 35 minutes.

(<u>Treadmill settings</u> / incline level 4 / speed level 3 mph)

Training frequency of week 10: minimum of 5 days

Week 11

Non Combo standard training (8-12 repetitions per set / 4-5 sets / 4-5 exercises of choice / light-moderate weight)

Concentration is on one major body part per day followed by (*treadmill) cardio*

60 minutes. (<u>Treadmill settings</u> / incline level 5 / speed level 3.7 mph)

Training frequency of week 11: minimum of 5 days

Week 12

(*Treadmill) cardio* no weight training

60 minutes. (<u>Treadmill settings</u> / incline level 5 / speed level 3.7 mph)

Training frequency of week 12: minimum of 6 days

This concludes the Level 2 / 12 week training program. In Level 2, every other week the training alternates between standard training and beginner combo training. Week 6 and week 12 focus only on cardio treadmill training. If you feel that Level 2 is easy for you, start out with a more difficult level. However, before jumping the gun into a higher level of training, completing weeks 10 and 11 from Level 2 is recommended for a self-fitness assessment. If in fact these two weeks are easy, you can move on to Level 3 training without sweat.

(Note) Be sure to maintain a healthy diet and eat food of good value.

(Level 3) Russian Conscript

Length of level 3 training (12 weeks)

<u>*Abdominals and calves*</u> *are to be trained twice a week, on days of choice before engaging in cardiovascular training.*

(No training of calves on weeks 4,8,12)

Week 1

Intermediate *Combo Training*

(15 repetitions per exercise light-weight) 4-5 combos

Concentration is on one major body part per day followed by (*treadmill*) *cardio* training of 50 minutes.

(<u>Treadmill settings</u> / incline level 3 / speed level 3 mph)

Training frequency of week 1: minimum of 5 days

Week 2

Non Combo standard training (8-12 repetitions per set / 5 sets / 4-5 exercises of choice / light-moderate weight)

Concentration is on one major body part per day followed by (*treadmill*) *cardio*

60 minutes. (<u>Treadmill settings</u> / incline level 6 / speed level 3.5 mph)

Training frequency of week 2: minimum of 5 days

Week 3

Intermediate *Combo Training*

(15 repetitions per exercise light-weight) 4-5 combos

Concentration is on one major body part per day followed by (*treadmill*) *cardio* training of 50 minutes.

(<u>Treadmill settings</u> / incline level 5 / speed level 3 mph)

Training frequency of week 3: minimum of 5 days

Week 4

Running

3-6 miles per run

Training frequency of week 4: minimum of 4 days/ maximum of 6 days

----

Week5

Non Combo standard training (8-12 repetitions per set / 5 sets / 4-5 exercises of choice / light-moderate weight)

Concentration is on one major body part per day followed by *(treadmill) cardio*

60 minutes. (Treadmill settings / incline level 3 / speed level 3.0 mph)

Training frequency of week 5: minimum of 5 days

Week 6

Intermediate *Combo Training*

(15 repetitions per exercise light-weight) 5 combos

Concentration is on one major body part per day followed by *(treadmill) cardio* **training of 55 minutes .**

(Treadmill settings / incline level 5 / speed level 3 mph)

Training frequency of week 5: minimum of 5 days

Week 7

Non Combo standard training (8-12 repetitions per set / 5 sets / 4-5 exercises of choice / light-moderate weight)

Concentration is on one major body part per day followed by *(treadmill) cardio*

60 minutes. (Treadmill settings / incline level 3 / speed level 3.0 mph)

Training frequency of week 7: minimum of 5 days

Week 8

Running

4-6 miles per run

Training frequency of week 8: minimum of 4 days/ maximum of 6 days

----

Week 9

Non Combo standard training (8-12 repetitions per set / 6 sets / 4-5 exercises of choice / light-moderate weight)

Concentration is on one major body part per day followed by (*treadmill*) *cardio*

60 minutes.(Treadmill settings / incline level 3 / speed level 3.0 mph)

Training frequency of week 9: minimum of 5 days

Week 10

Intermediate *Combo Training*

(15 repetitions per exercise light-weight) 6 combos

Concentration is on one major body part per day followed by (*treadmill*) *cardio* training of 40 minutes.

(Treadmill settings / incline level 6 / speed level 4 mph)

Training frequency of week 10: minimum of 5 days

Week 11

Intermediate *Combo Training*

(15 repetitions per exercise light-weight) 6 combos

Concentration is on one major body part per day followed by (*treadmill*) *cardio* training of 40 minutes.

(Treadmill settings / incline level 8 / speed level 4 mph)

Training frequency of week 11: minimum of 5 days

Week 12

Running

5-6 miles per run

Training frequency of week 12: minimum of 4 days/ maximum of 6 days

Hands down any Comrade who can go through Level 3 while maintaining healthy food habits can look forward to continuous results. After week 12 of Level 3 training, the Comrade can take it easy for a few days before starting week 1 of Level 4 training.

"Congratulations Comrade! Upon finishing Level 3 you are no longer considered to be at a conscript training level in glorious Soviet motherland Russia.

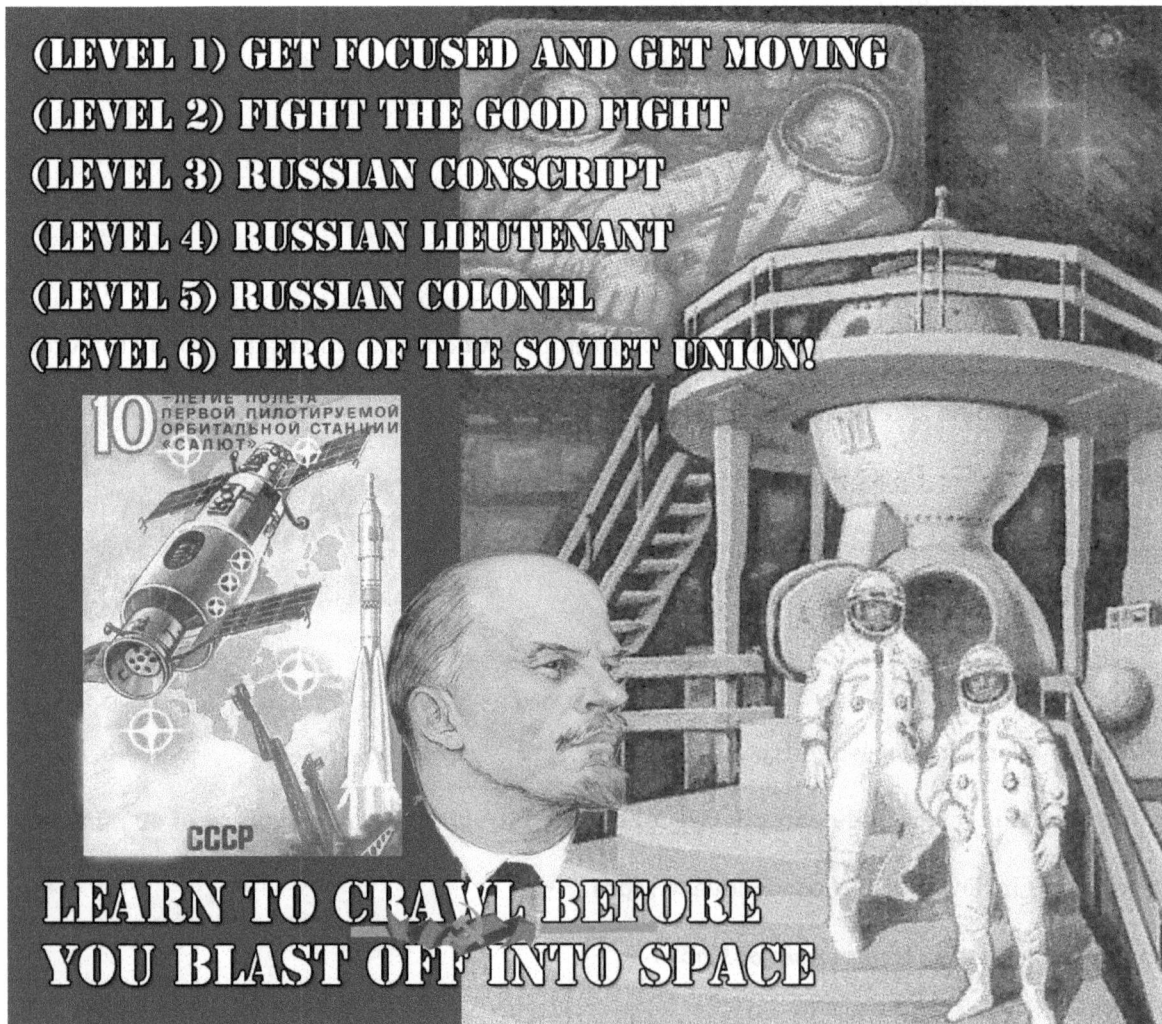

(Level 4) Russian Lieutenant

Length of level 3 training (12 weeks)

<u>*Abdominals and calves*</u> *are to be trained three times a week on days of choice before engaging in cardiovascular training.*

(No training of calves on week 4,8,12)

Week 1

Intermediate *Combo Training*

(15 repetitions per exercise light-weight) 4-5 combos

Concentration is on one major body part per day followed by (*stairmaster*) *cardio* training of 50 minutes.

(<u>Stairmaster settings</u> / speed level 3)

Training frequency of week 1: minimum of 5 days

Week 2

Non Combo standard training (8-12 repetitions per set / 5 sets / 4-5 exercises of choice / light-moderate weight)

Concentration is on one major body part per day followed by (*stairmaster*) *cardio*

50 minutes. (<u>Stairmaster settings</u> / speed level 3)

Training frequency of week 2: minimum of 5 days

Week 3

Intermediate *Combo Training*

(15 repetitions per exercise light-weight) 4-5 combos

Concentration is on one major body part per day followed by (*stairmaster*) *cardio* training of 50 minutes.

(<u>Stairmaster settings</u> / speed level 3)

Training frequency of week 3: minimum of 5 days

Week 4

Running

4-6 miles per run

Training frequency of week 4: minimum of 4 days/ maximum of 6 days

----

Week 5

Non Combo standard training (8-12 repetitions per set / 5 sets / 4-5 exercises of choice / light-moderate weight)

Concentration is on one major body part per day followed by (*stairmaster***) cardio**

60 minutes. (Stairmaster settings / speed level 3)

5 days a week

Week 6

Intermediate *Combo Training*

(15 repetitions per exercise light-weight) 5 combos

Concentration is on one major body part per day followed by (*stairmaster***) cardio training of 50 minutes.**

(Stairmaster settings / speed level 3)

Training frequency of week 6: minimum of 5 days

Week 7

Non Combo standard training (8-12 repetitions per set / 5 sets / 4-5 exercises of choice / light-moderate weight)

Concentration is on one major body part per day followed by (*stairmaster***) cardio**

60 minutes.(Stairmaster settings / speed level 3)

Training frequency of week 7: minimum of 5 days

Week 8
Running
6 days

- Monday) Day1- (2miles)
- Tuesday) Day2 - (6miles)
- Wednesday) Day3 – (2miles)
- Thursday) Day4 - (8 miles)
- Friday) Day 5 - (2 miles)
- Saturday) Day 6 – (10 miles)
- Sunday) Day 7 - Off

Week 9

Non Combo standard training (8-12 repetitions per set / 6 sets / 4-5 exercises of choice / light-moderate weight)

Concentration is on one major body part per day followed by (*stairmaster*) *cardio*

60 minutes. (Stairmaster settings / speed level 4.0)

Training frequency of week 9: minimum of 5 days

Week 10

Intermediate *Combo Training*

(15 repetitions per exercise light-weight) 6 combos

Concentration is on one major body part per day followed by (*stairmaster*) *cardio* training of 50 minutes.

(Stairmaster settings / speed level 4 mph)

Training frequency of week 10: minimum of 5 days

Week 11

Intermediate *Combo Training*

(15 repetitions per exercise light-weight) 6 combos

Concentration is on one major body part per day followed by (*stairmaster*) *cardio* training of 50 minutes.

(Stairmaster settings / speed level 4 mph)

Training frequency of week 11: minimum of 5 days

--254----------------------

Week 12
Running
6 days

- **Monday) Day1- (3miles)**
- **Tuesday) Day2 – (6miles)**
- **Wednesday) Day3 – (3miles)**
- **Thursday) Day4 – (9 miles)**
- **Friday) Day 5 – (3 miles)**
- **Saturday) Day 6 – (12 miles)**
- **Sunday) Day 7 - Off**

A Comrade who survives Levels 2 - 4 is a Comrade who will be in glorious shape if a nutritious diet was maintained during the training. There is no need to continue to Level 5 if you already attained the goal you were striving to achieve. Simple maintenance work should keep you in check. However, if you want to challenge yourself further and have a first-hand experience of what the Soviet Russian generals go through on a daily basis, Level 5 is next. "Long live glorious Level 5."

URA! URA! URA!

(Level 5) Russian Colonel

Length of level 5 training (8 weeks)

<u>Abdominals and calves</u> *are to be trained four times a week on days of choice before engaging in cardiovascular training.*

(No training of calves on week 2,4,7)

Week 1

Advanced *Combo Training*

- *(18 repetitions per exercise light-weight) 5 combos*

Concentration is on one major body part per day followed by (*stairmaster*) *cardio* training of 60 minutes.

<u>(Stairmaster settings</u> / speed level 4)

Training frequency of week 1: minimum of 5 days

Week 2
Running
6 days

- Monday) Day1- (3miles)
- Tuesday) Day2 – (6miles)
- Wednesday) Day3 – (3miles)
- Thursday) Day4 – (9 miles)
- Friday) Day 5 – (3 miles)
- Saturday) Day 6 – (12 miles)
- Sunday) Day 7 – Off

Week 3

Advanced *Combo Training*

- *(18 repetitions per exercise light-weight) 6 combos*

Concentration is on one major body part per day followed by (*stairmaster*) *cardio* training of 60 minutes.

<u>(Stairmaster settings</u> / speed level 4)

Training frequency of week 3: minimum of 5 days

Week 4
Running
6 days

- Monday) Day1- (4miles)
- Tuesday) Day2 – (8miles)
- Wednesday) Day3 – (4miles)
- Thursday) Day4 – (12 miles)
- Friday) Day 5 – (2 miles)
- Saturday) Day 6 – (16 miles)
- Sunday) Day 7 – Off

Week 5

***The Crazies *Combo Training*

- *(20 repetitions per exercise light-weight) 6 combos*

Concentration is on one major body part per day followed by (*stairmaster*) *cardio* training of 60 minutes.

(Stairmaster settings / speed level 5)

Training frequency of week 5: minimum of 5 days

Week 6

Advanced *Combo Training*

- *(18 repetitions per exercise light-weight) 5 combos*

Concentration is on one major body part per day followed by (*stairmaster*) *cardio* training of 60 minutes.

(Stairmaster settings / speed level 5)

Training frequency of week 6: minimum of 5 days

Week 7

Running
6 days

- **Monday) Day1- (2miles)**
- **Tuesday) Day2 – (10miles)**
- **Wednesday) Day3 – (2miles)**
- **Thursday) Day4 – (10 miles)**
- **Friday) Day 5 – (2 miles)**
- **Saturday) Day 6 – (20 miles)**
- **Sunday) Day 7 – Off**

Week 8

***The Crazies *Combo Training*

- *(20 repetitions per exercise light-weight) 6 combos*

Concentration is on one major body part per day followed by (*stairmaster) cardio* training of 60 minutes.

(Stairmaster settings / speed level 6)

Training frequency of week 8: minimum of 6 days

You might ask who would ever want to do Level 5 training. The answer is Movie stars, models, business executives, CEOs and any other Comrade who wants to stand apart from other Comrades.

As far as Level 6, it's designed for crazy Comrades who like to train in an unorthodox fashion. Level 6 is extremely rugged, aggressive and unconventional. Any Comrade who is thinking about joining the Special Forces or wants to become a rugged MMA fighter, Level 6 is specifically geared towards that direction. Please reference chapter 18 after looking over the Level 6 (4 week training program). Level 6 should not be followed for longer than 4 weeks at a time.

(Note) If the Comrade finishes the (Level 6, 4 week training program,) it is highly recommended that he or she take at least one week off from training to recover.

WARNING!!!!!!!

Level 6 is for entertainment and knowledge purposes only.

Be sure to check with your doctor and have full clearance prior to training and committing to any serious workout/training program. Not all training programs fit all individuals. The author and his affiliates do not take any responsibility for any injuries or deaths that may occur in any physical training program. The information in this book is written for entertainment and knowledge purposes only. Any individual following any programs from Russian Ripped does so at his/her own risk after being released by a doctor to do so.

(Level 6) Hero of the Soviet Union!
Please reference chapter 18

Week1
Day1) In Soviet Russia Bag Hit You (2 hours)
Day 2) Kettle Bleachers and Laps (4 miles)
Day 3) The Spetsnaz Pullup Squat, Pushup Special (301 combos)
Day 4) The Stalin 301 (2 hours) followed by a 10 mile run
Day 5) The Putin 301 (2 hours)
Day 6) The 9th Company Drags (set no of hill climbs) followed by a 10 mile run
Day 7 off-----

Week2
Day1) In Soviet Russia Bag Hit You (3 hours) followed by a 10 mile run
Day 2) Kettle Bleachers and Laps (5 miles)
Day 3) The Spetsnaz Pullup Squat, Pushup Special (301 combos)
Day 4) The Stalin 301 (3 hours) followed by a 10 mile run
Day 5) The Putin 301 (3 hours)
Day 6) The 9th Company Drags (set no of hill climbs) followed by a 10 mile run
Day 7 off-----

Week3
Day1) In Soviet Russia Bag Hit You (2 hours) 10 mile run
Day 2) Kettle Bleachers and Laps (4 miles)
Day 3) The Spetsnaz Pullup Squat, Pushup Special (301 combos)
Day 4) The Stalin 301 (2 hours) followed by a 10 mile run
Day 5) The Putin 301 (2 hours) followed by a 10 mile run
Day 6) The 9th Company Drags (set no of hill climbs) followed by a 10 mile run
Day 7 off-----

Week4
Day1) In Soviet Russia Bag Hit You (4 hours) followed by a 10 mile run
Day 2) Kettle Bleachers and Laps (6 miles)
Day 3) The Spetsnaz Pullup Squat, Pushup Special (301 combos)
Day 4) The Stalin 301 (4 hours) followed by a 10 mile run
Day 5) The Putin 301 (4 hours) followed by a 10 mile run
Day 6) The 9th Company Drags (set no of hill climbs) followed by a 2 mile run
Day 7) 20 mile run

Any Comrade who is interested in joining the Special Forces can attain a clear understanding as to where he or she stands through the Level 6 training approach. The Comrade who completes Level 6 training without cheating, is probably one of the toughest Comrades who can comfortably fight: 10 hungry bears, 20 crazy wolves, 30 vicious snow leopards and 300 Spartans all at the same time, while bench pressing 315lbs with one hand and curling a heavy dumbbell in the other.

Chapter 18 – The Renegade Soviet Special Forces Comrade Training Option

Welcome to unconventional training Comrades. Enjoy

In Soviet Russia, Bag Hit You!

1) Grab a punching bag and a stop watch.

2) Find a challenging hill.

3) Keep count of how many times you can make it up and down the hill in 1 hour with the punching bag. You must carry the bag! No dragging the bag on the ground Comrade.

4) Going up and down the hill counts as one completion.

5) Once you come back down the hill, perform 25 full body squats and 25 pushups. If necessary, break up the squats and pushups to reach a total of 50 repetitions. **(Note)** If you can't do proper pushups and full body squats, you are not ready for this exercise.

6) For the real crazies; perform 10-25 of the squats without putting the punching bag down.

(Note) This exercise is not intended to be comfortable. Switching up bag positions from shoulder to shoulder every few minutes is advised.

(Note) Hilly terrain is known for twisting ankles. The second a Comrade stops paying attention to where the foot lands, the chances of rolling or twisting an ankle amplify significantly. (I am guilty of this and it was painful so watch out).

(Notes) Be hydrated and if possible bring someone along. If no one is going with you, have a phone on you at all times and tell a few people where you will be in case of an emergency.

FIND A GOOD HILL TO RUN AND GRAB A PUNCHING BAG.

#1

IN SOVIET RUSSIA BAG HIT YOU!

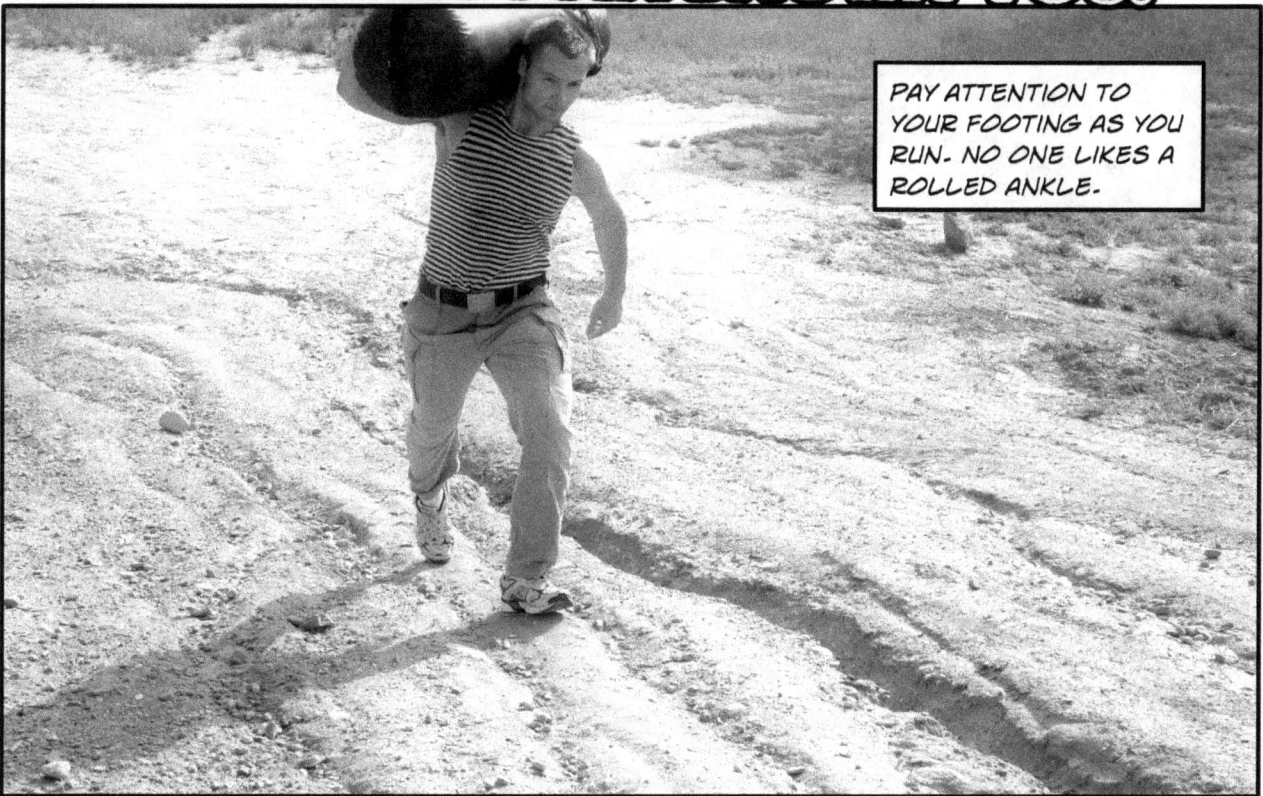

PAY ATTENTION TO YOUR FOOTING AS YOU RUN. NO ONE LIKES A ROLLED ANKLE.

RUN UP THE HILL AND LET THOSE LEGS BURN!

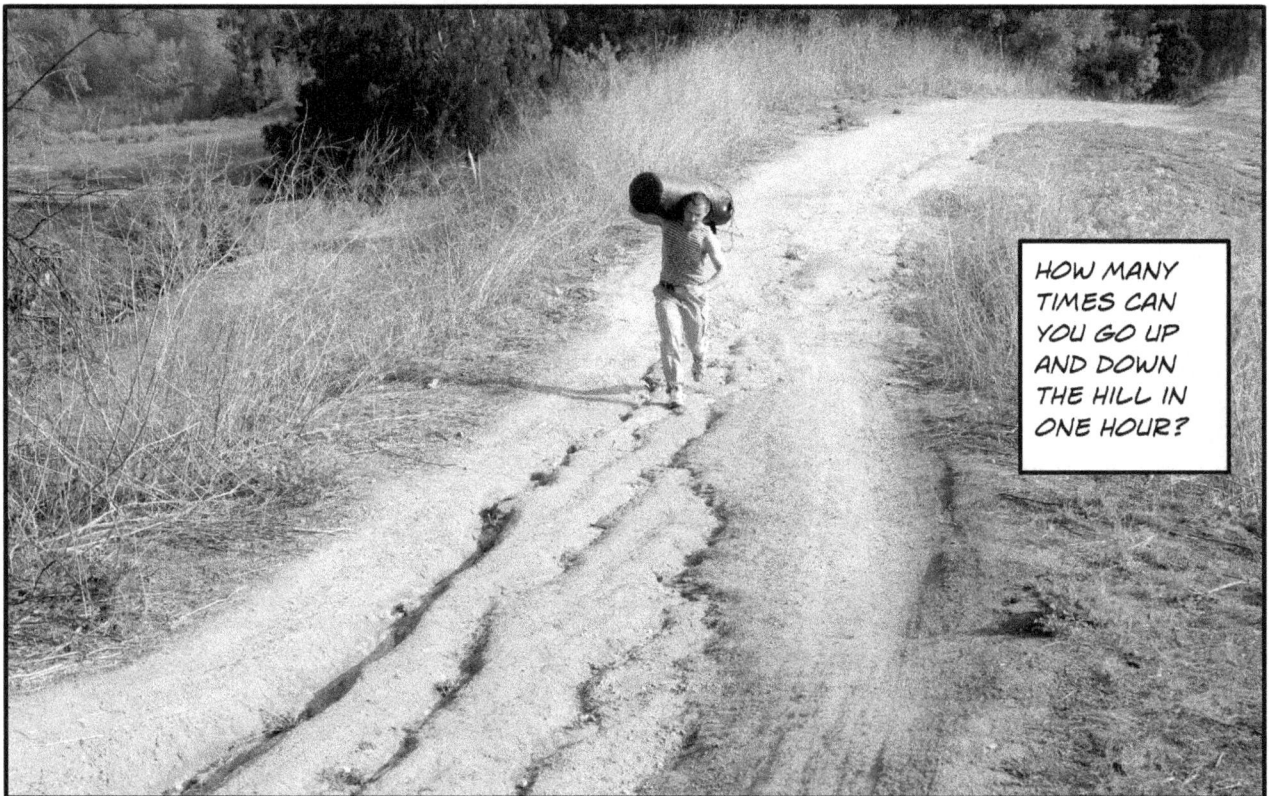

HOW MANY TIMES CAN YOU GO UP AND DOWN THE HILL IN ONE HOUR?

AS SOON AS YOU COME BACK DOWN THE HILL START TO SQUAT. (25 SQUATS TOTAL). IT'S OPTIONAL TO SQUAT WITH OR WITHOUT THE PUNCHING BAG.

#2

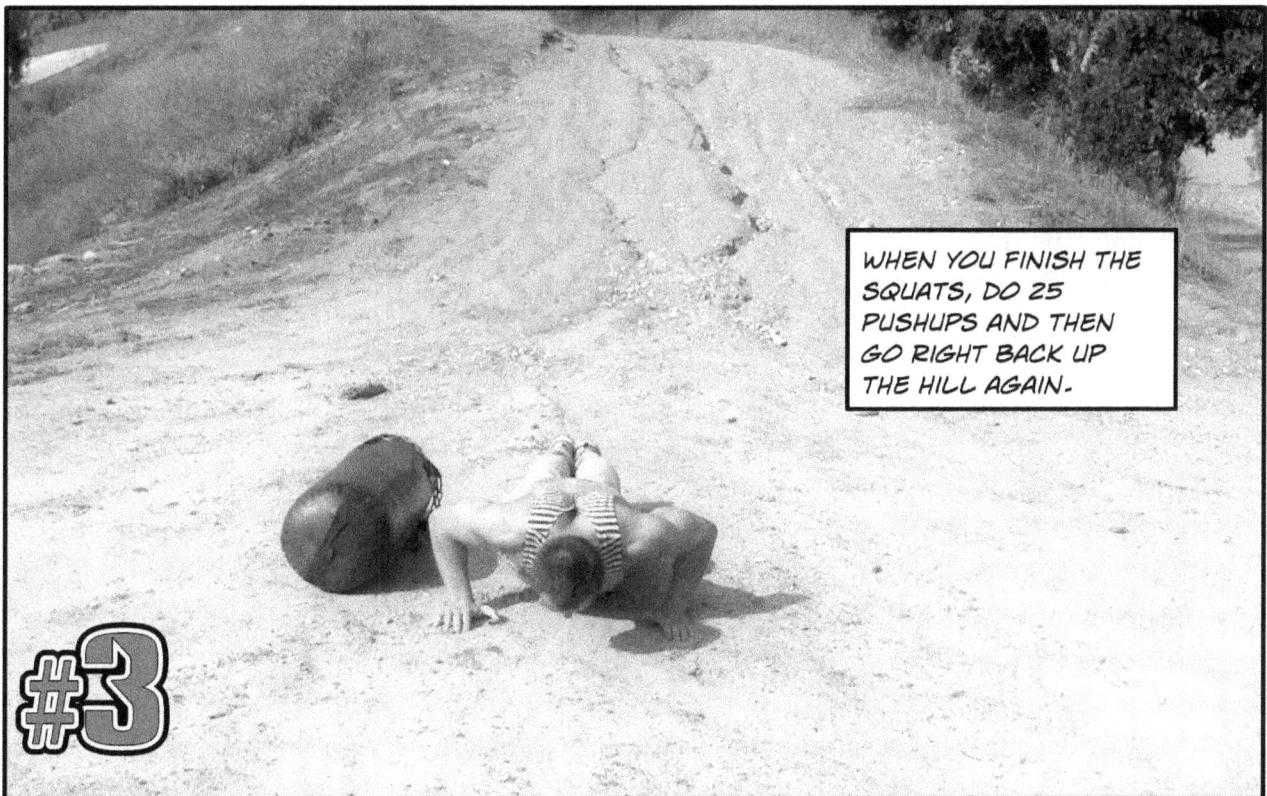

WHEN YOU FINISH THE SQUATS, DO 25 PUSHUPS AND THEN GO RIGHT BACK UP THE HILL AGAIN.

#3

Kettle Bleachers and Laps

This exercise is limited as to where it may be performed. Usually, a high school campus with solid concrete bleachers works great.

(Note) This exercise combination requires proper balance. Any Comrade with problems in the balance department should avoid this exercise.

In Soviet Russia this exercise is widely prescribed by doctors for people who talk a lot about their awesomeness fitness level. Soviet Russian definition states that: awesomeness is only attained after the Comrade finishes 20 completions from the "Kettle Bleachers and Laps" workout routine.

1) Place a kettlebell on the first step of the bleachers by the entrance.

2) The starting running position should be by the middle entrance of the bleachers.

3) Run one lap at moderate or fast speed.

4) Grab the kettle bell and step squat up the stairs slowly. Always lean forward when squatting up. It's a long way down if you fall!

5) Immediately as you reach the top, turn around with the kettlebell and squat back down with a split second sit down on each step. Rest the kettlebell one step bellow on every squat. Lift with the legs not the back.

6) Immediately do 10 pushups when you come back down to the running track and start running the next lap.

7) Keep doing this until you can work up to 20 laps. (5 miles). It's common to only do a few laps the first time around before the body starts to go into shut down mode. If you feel weak, stop immediately.

(Note) Running one lap, doing the bleacher squats, and pushups counts as one completion.

5 completions = Spartan wannabe
10 completions = Spartan
15 completions = Soviet Russian wannabe
20 completions = Soviet spirit awesomeness embodies you Comrade
20 completions with two kettlebells = Hero of Soviet Russia

(Note) Be hydrated and if possible bring someone along. If no one is going with you, have a phone on you at all times and tell a few people where you will be in case of an emergency.

PLACE A KETTLE-BELL ON THE FIRST STEP OF THE BLEACHERS BY THE ENTRANCE.

KETTLE BLEACHERS AND LAPS

#1

RUN ONE LAP AT A MODERATE OR FAST PACE.

#2

STEP UP

#3

SQUAT

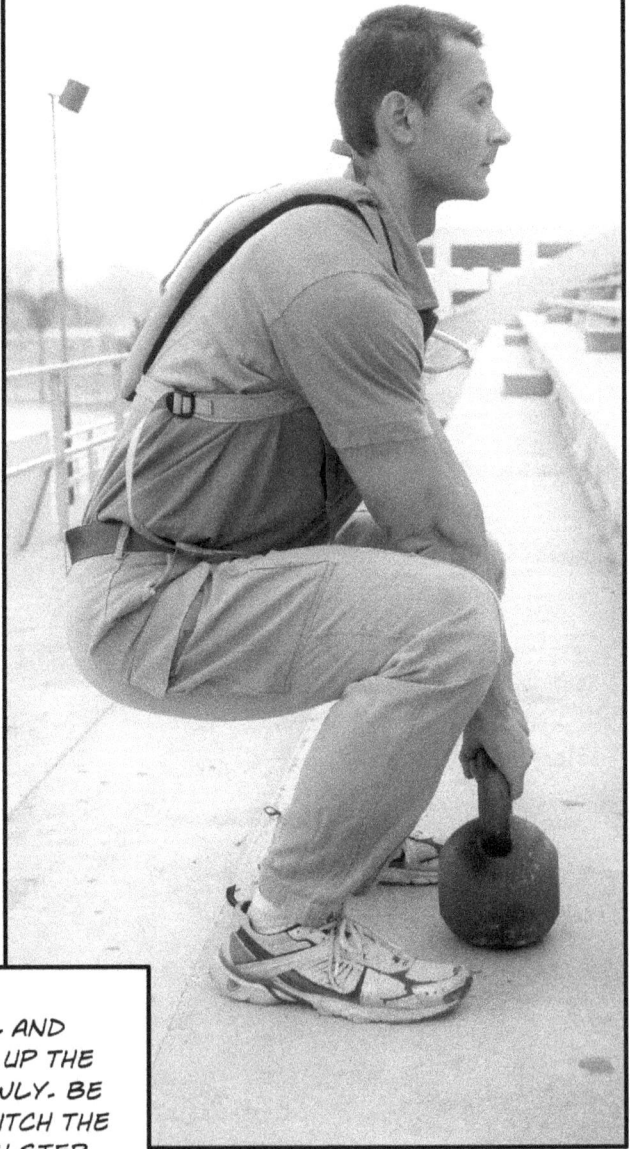

GRAB THE KETTLEBELL AND STEP SQUAT UP THE STAIRS SLOWLY. BE SURE TO SWITCH THE LEGS AS YOU STEP UP. ALWAYS LEAN FORWARD WHEN SQUATTING UP.

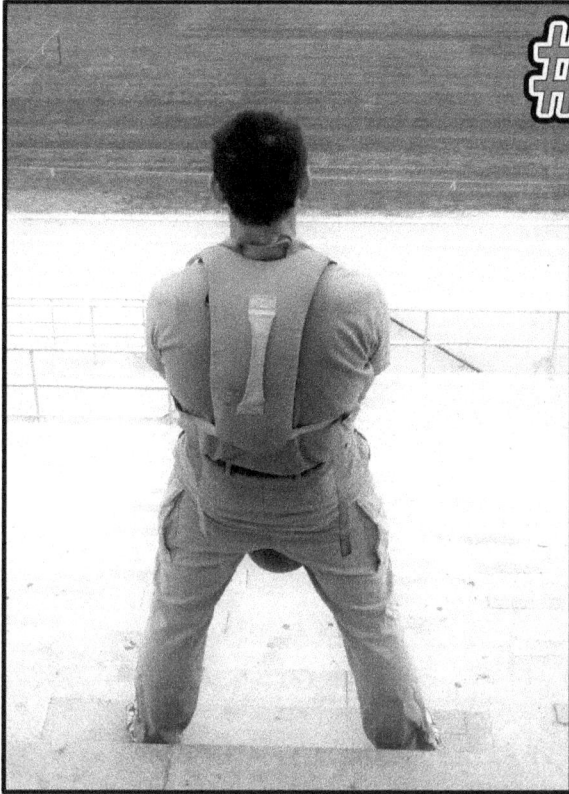

#4

WHEN YOU GET TO THE TOP OF THE BLEACHERS:
1) TURN AROUND AND SQUAT DOWN. PLACE THE KETTLEBELL DOWN ONE STEP BELOW BETWEEN THE LEGS.
2) STAND UP, TAKE ONE STEP DOWN AND SQUAT DOWN AGAIN. CONTINUE DOING THIS ALL THE WAY TO THE BOTTOM OF THE BLEACHERS. EXHALE AS YOU SQUAT UP AND INHALE AS YOU SQUAT DOWN.

#5

STARTING POSITION
(1)

SQUAT DOWN (2)

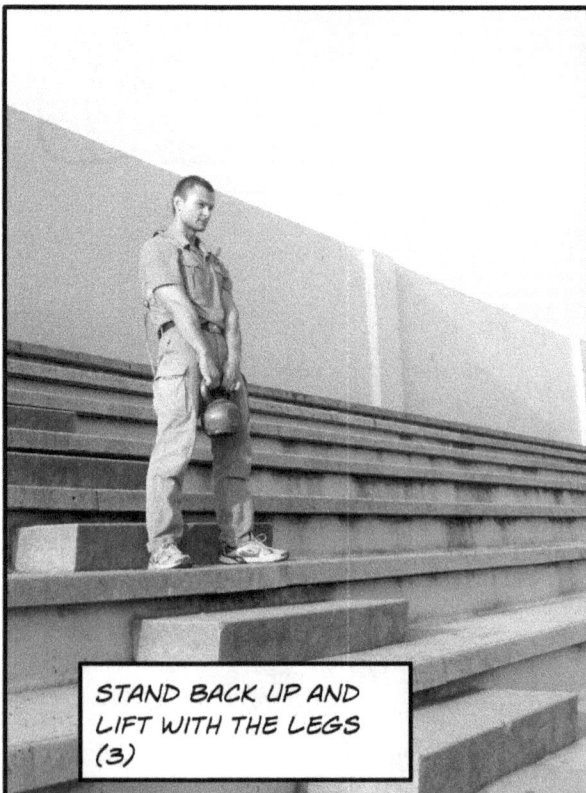

STAND BACK UP AND
LIFT WITH THE LEGS
(3)

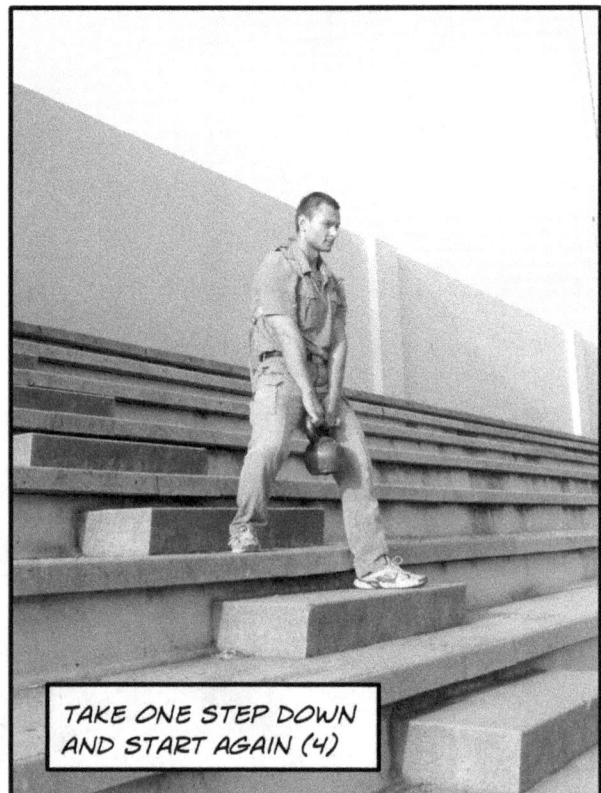

TAKE ONE STEP DOWN
AND START AGAIN (4)

#6

IMMEDIATELY DO 10 PUSHUPS WHEN YOU COME DOWN TO THE TRACK AND START RUNNING THE NEXT LAP.

The Spetsnaz Pullup Squat, Pushup Special
I have personally witnessed several Comrades practically die on this exercise.
Any Comrade who can reach 301 completions in a training session under 120 minutes is considered to be a Hero of Soviet Russia. In the beginning start out with a few completions and gradually work your way up.

When starting, stand directly underneath the pullup bar with two dumbbells on the floor by the side of each leg.

Beginner
Standard combined dumbbell weight around 10% of body weight. If a Comrade weighs 200 lbs that's 10lb dumbbell on each side (200 x .1 = 20 lbs)

Warrior
Standard combined dumbbell weight around 15% of body weight. If a Comrade weighs 200 lbs that's 15lb dumbbell on each side (200 x .15 = 30lbs)

Hero
Standard combined dumbbell weight around 20% of body weight. If a Comrade weighs 200 lbs that's 20lb dumbbell on each side (200 x .2 = 40lbs)

Super Soviet Russian Hero
Standard combined dumbbell weight around 40% of body weight. If a Comrade weighs 200 lbs that's 40lb dumbbell on each side (200 x .4 = 80lbs)

Lady Comrades may have a bench on the side by the pullup bar to assist in doing leg-push pullups. (Pushing off with the toes as the pull up is preformed).

1) Perform a full range pull up of any version.

2) Come down with control and free squat down to the dumbbells.

3) Grab hold of the dumbbells, exhale and come up with the dumbbells to a fully standing position.

4) Come back down all the way into a deep squat position. Place the dumbbells on the sides. Jump or extend the legs back while leaning on the handles of the dumbbells and perform a pushup.

5) Jump back to the deep squat position, let go of the dumbbells and come up for the next pullup.

This sequence counts as one completion.

#1

STARTING POSITION- STAND DIRECTLY UNDER THE PULLUP BAR WITH TWO DUMBBELLS ON THE SIDES.

THE SPETSNAZ PULL-UP SQUAT, PUSHUP SPECIAL

#2

GRAB ON TO THE PULLUP BAR TO PERFORM ANY VARIATION OF A FULL RANGE PULLUP.

#3

PERFORM THE PULLUP

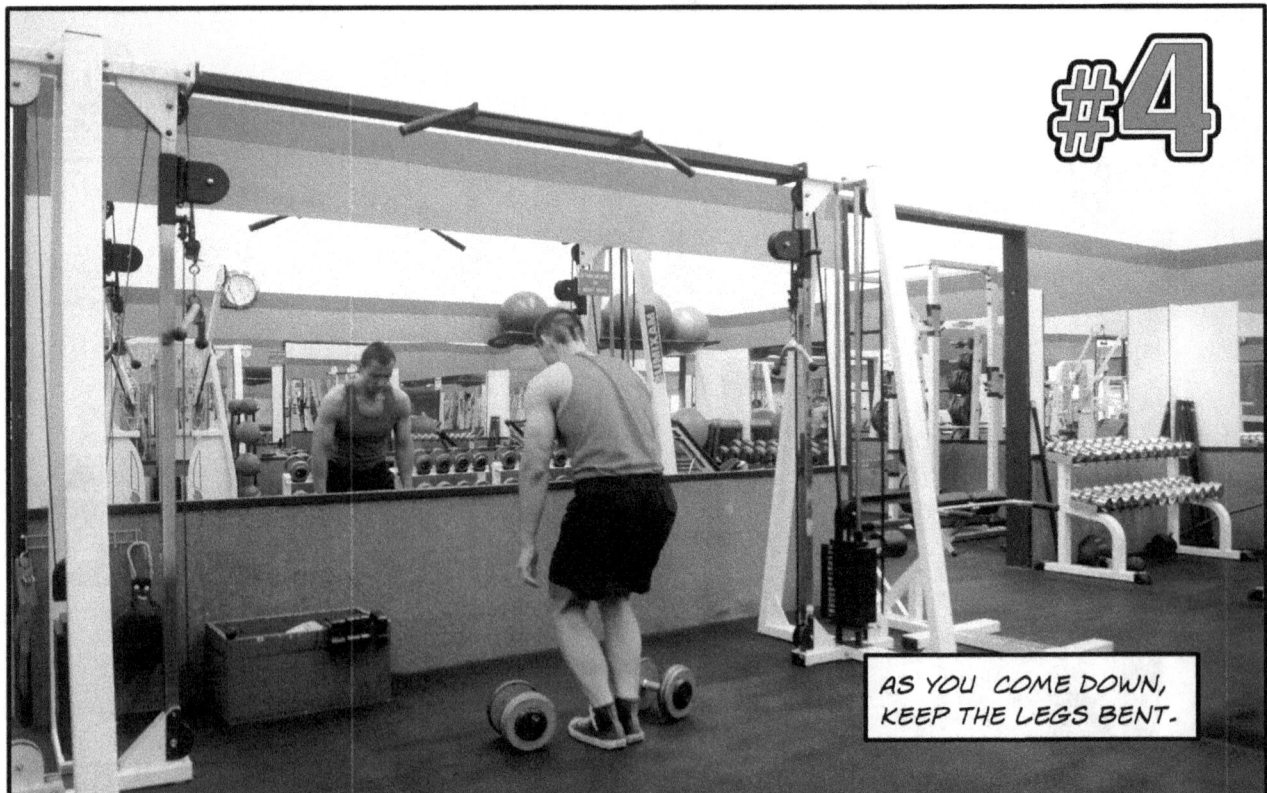

#4

AS YOU COME DOWN,
KEEP THE LEGS BENT.

COME DOWN TO A DEEP SQUAT POSITION, GRAB THE DUMBBELLS AND COME UP. BE SURE TO EXHALE AS YOU COME UP WITHT THE WEIGHT.

#5

COME UP AND FLEX THE LEGS

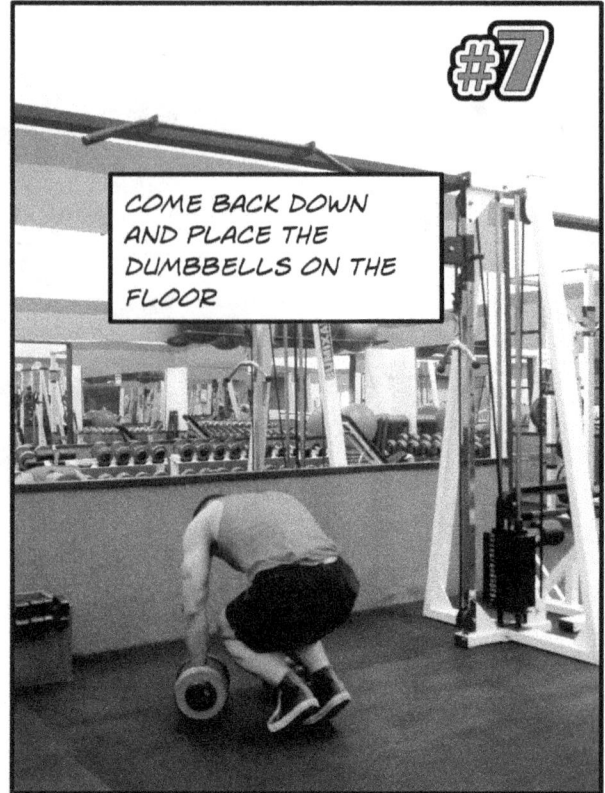

COME BACK DOWN AND PLACE THE DUMBBELLS ON THE FLOOR

JUMP BACK AND HOLD THE PUSHUP POSITION ON THE DUMBBELLS

PERFORM A PUSHUP

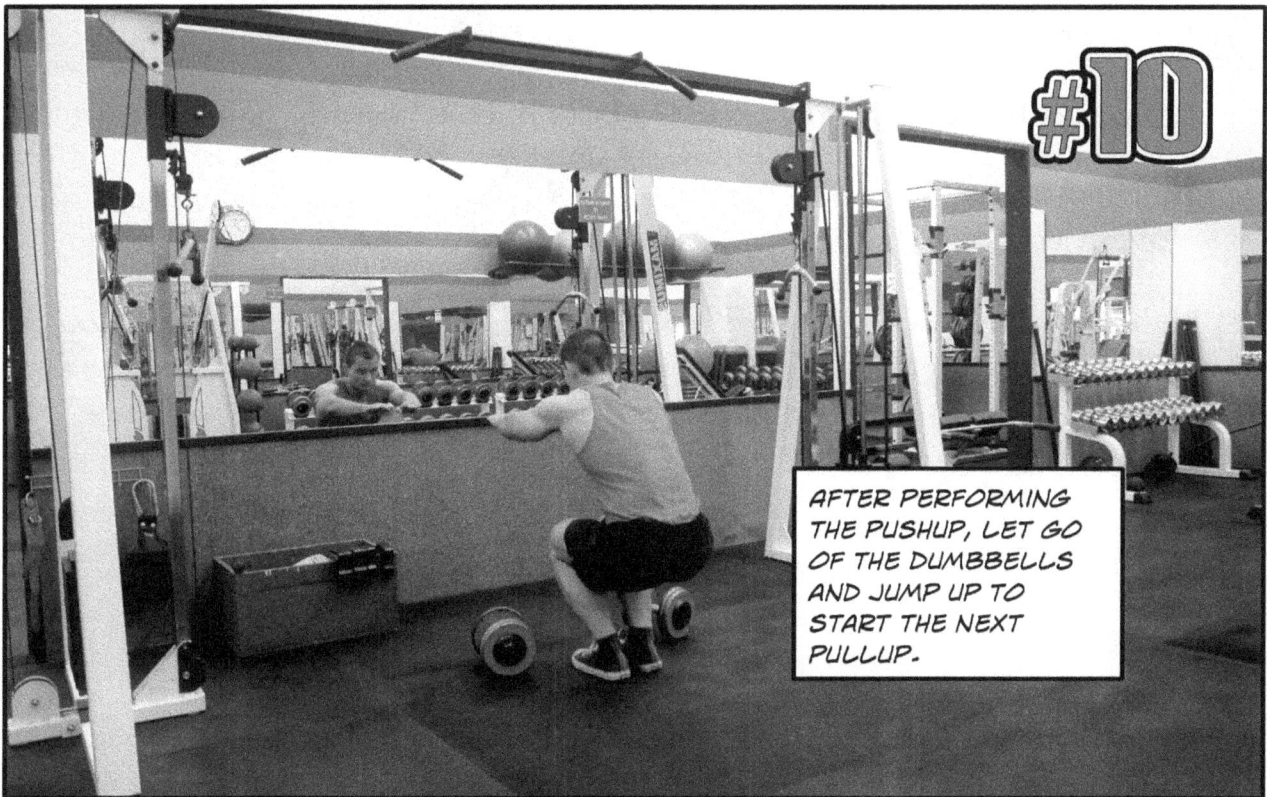

#10

AFTER PERFORMING THE PUSHUP, LET GO OF THE DUMBBELLS AND JUMP UP TO START THE NEXT PULLUP.

The Stalin 301

This exercise is called the Stalin 301 because Stalin didn't think that number 300 was sufficient. Actually, Once in the 1950's, 301 Soviet Russian soldiers withstood the onslaught of the crazy experimental self-cloning Soviet Stalin Russian Zombie machines in the Moscow metro system. Saving all humanity from doom and even saving one lost Spartan who was hiding in an unusually narrow corridor. Since then, the number 301 became famous. You laugh now, but wait till the exercise starts and laughing will become but a distant memory.

Take 2 kettle bells of the same weight and find a long hill, preferably with a dirt road going up. The starting position is at the bottom of the hill.

1) While holding a pushup position with both hands on the kettle bells, swing one kettle bell forward. Keep the abdominals tight.

2) Shift the body weight on to the front kettlebell at the same time as you swing the back kettlebell forward.

3) Jump in with the legs, exhale and squat up.

4) Squat back down, shift the weight back on the kettlebells, jump back and repeat the process.

This counts as one completion.

Try practicing on a flat surface and be careful not to roll the kettlebell on its side. Rolling the kettlebell may hurt the wrist. The roll usually happens when balance is lost. Any Comrade who can reach 301 completions in a training session without a set time limit is considered to be a Hero of Soviet Russia.

(Note) Be hydrated and if possible take someone along. If no one is going with you, have a phone on you at all times and tell a few people where you will be in case of an emergency.

#1

STARTING POSITION

THE STALIN 301

#2

SWING ONE ARM FORWARD. ALWAYS KEEP THE ABBS TIGHT.

#3

SWING THE OTHER
ARM FORWARD

#4

STABILIZE THE NEW
POSITION

#5

JUMP IN WITH BOTH LEGS

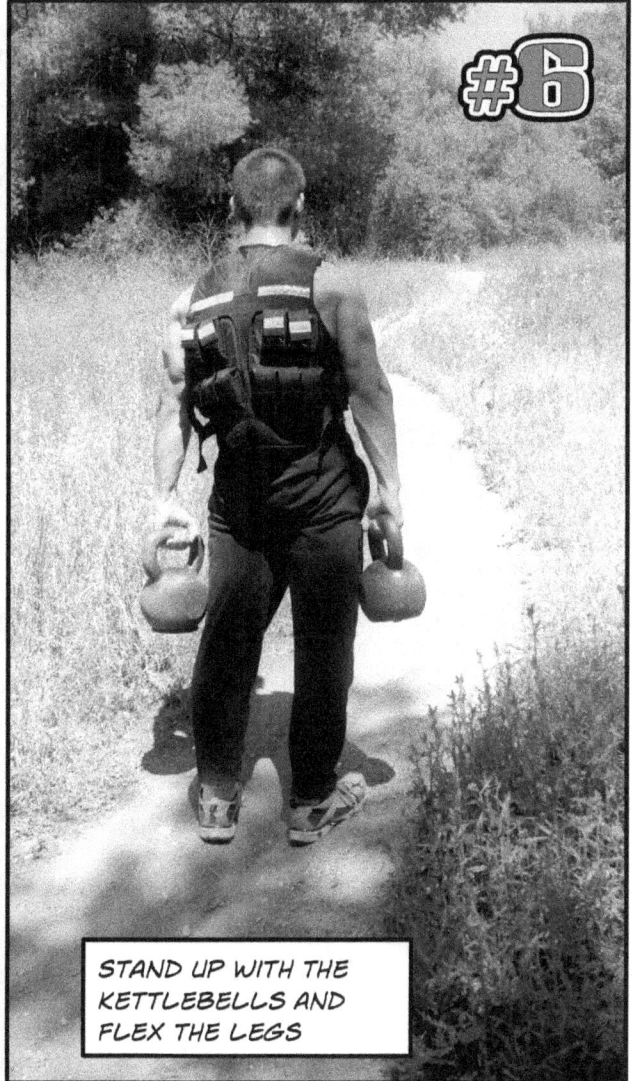

#6

STAND UP WITH THE KETTLEBELLS AND FLEX THE LEGS

#7

SQUAT DOWN, JUMP BACK IN TO THE PUSHUP POSITION AND CONTINUE ON TO THE NEXT SET.

IF THE HILL YOU CHOOSE IS UNEVEN AND STEEP, THE EXERCISE BECOMES MUCH HARDER. TRY PRACTICING ON EVEN GROUND FIRST.

The Putin 301

The Putin 301 is designed to annihilate the Comrades glorious behind and legs. It's an exercise that Comrades in general don't like. However, this exercise is the mother Russian standard for sculpting the butt through an unconventional approach.

Take 2 dumbbells or kettlebells of the same weight and find a suitable hill, preferably with a dirt road. The starting position is at the bottom of the hill.

1) On the Inhale, perform a deep squat with both legs close together. The behind is to make contact with the calves.

2) Exhale and squat back up.

3) Lunge forward with the right leg (keeping the back straight).

4) Pull the back leg in.

5) Exhale and squat up.

6) Lunge deep with the left (keeping the back straight).

7) Pull the back leg in.

8) Exhale and squat up.

A deep lunge with each leg and 2 deep squats counts as one completion. Any Comrade, who can complete 301 completions in one training session under 2 hours without cheating, is considered to be a Hero of Soviet Motherland Russia. Please, for the love of everything that is holy, if you have a bad knee joint or can not perform deep lunges for other health reasons do not do this exercise.

(Note) Be hydrated and if possible bring someone along. If no one is going with you, have a phone on you at all times and tell a few people where you will be in case of an emergency.

#1 STARTING POSITION

THE PUTIN 301

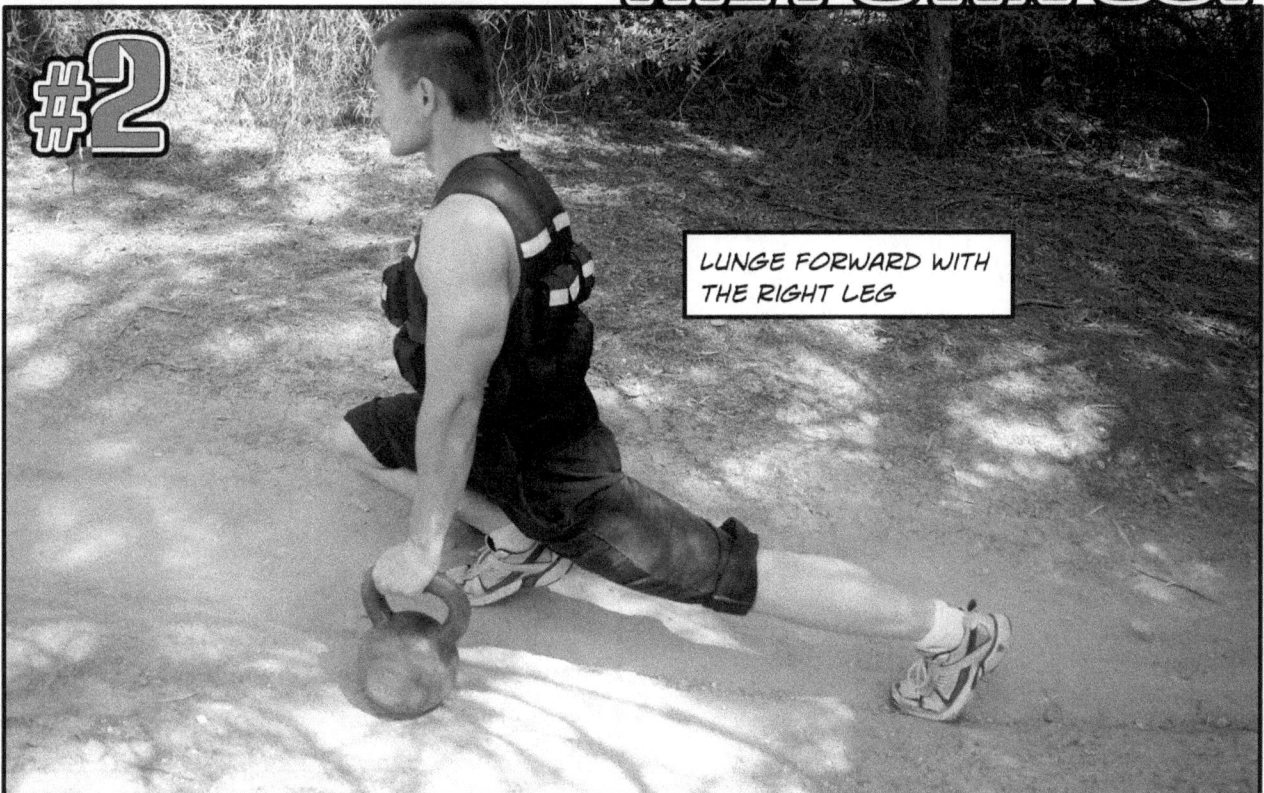

#2 LUNGE FORWARD WITH THE RIGHT LEG

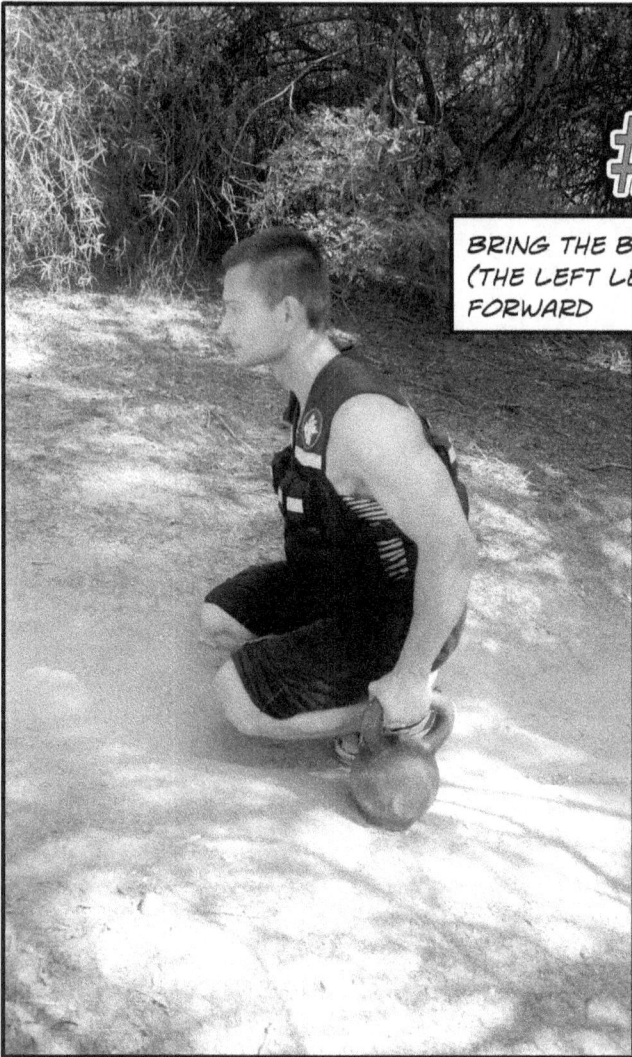

#3

BRING THE BACK LEG (THE LEFT LEG) FORWARD

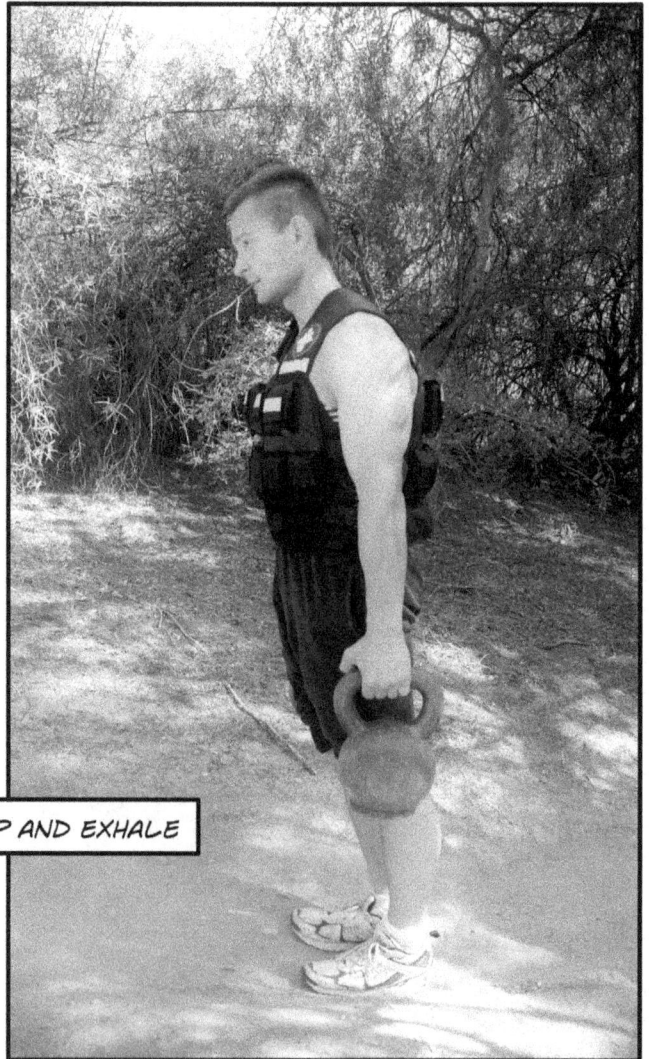

#4

STAND UP AND EXHALE

#5

LUNGE FORWARD
WITHT HE LEFT LEG

#6

BRING THE BACK LEG
FORWARD (THE RIGHT
LEG)

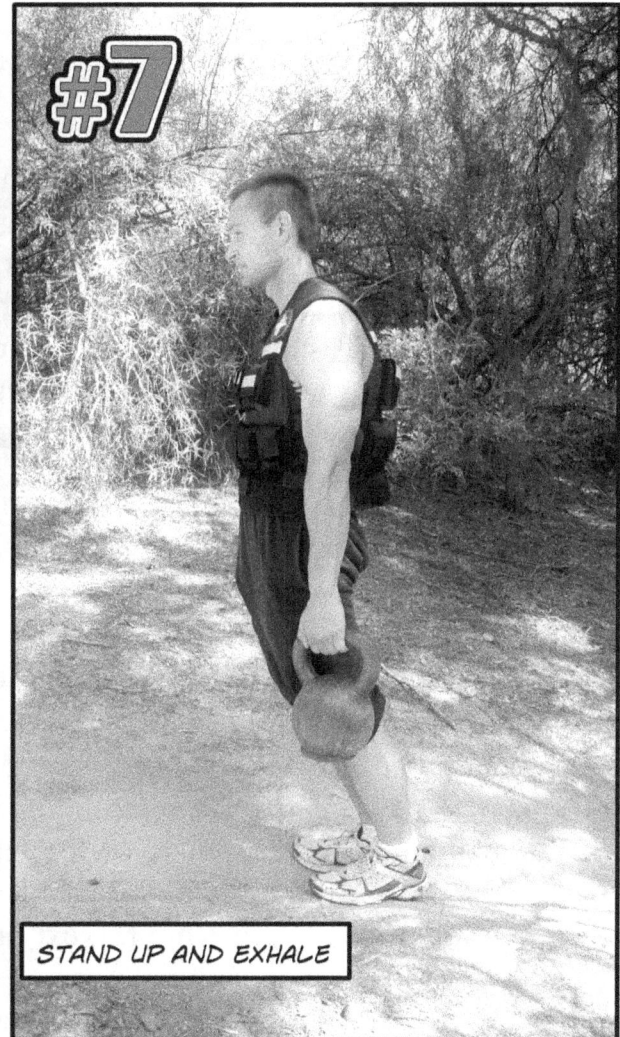

#7

STAND UP AND EXHALE

The 9th Company Drags

Beginner

1 hour of continuous training

Warrior

2 hours of continuous training

Hero

3 hours of continuous training

Super Soviet Russian Hero

4 hours of continuous training

I have seen more Comrades lose their lunch on this exercise than on any other exercise in this chapter. It's quite possible because I was yelling at them and not letting them rest, but we shall not bring up the past. For this exercise you will need a weight vest, a long chain or a good rope, some sturdy gloves and a heavy weight that can be tied off and dragged. A weight plate is considered to be the easiest drag due to its smooth surface. A kettlebell is one of the hardest drag weights because it twists and turns making it unpredictable and difficult to control. This is not football Comrades leave the mini parachutes and weight dragging sleds at home.

After you tie off the weight, grab on to the end of the chain or rope. You are free to drag the weight up the hill in any manner as long as you do not carry it.

(Note) Having at least 6-12 feet between you and the drag weight is recommended.
(Note) Don't let dehydration ruin your vacation.
(Note) Going up and down the hill counts as one full completion so don't get exited when you reach the top because you still need to go down.
(Note) This is an amazingly difficult workout if it's executed on a sand hill.
(Note) When the weights get stuck, or the legs start giving out, sit down, turn around and row the weight up using the arms and back muscles. Keep count of how many times you make it up and down the hill in 1 hour. Next time you come back to The 9th Company Drags try to beat the previous number of hill climbs.
(Notes) Be hydrated and if possible bring someone along. If no one is going with you, have a phone on you at all times and tell a few people where you will be in case of an emergency.

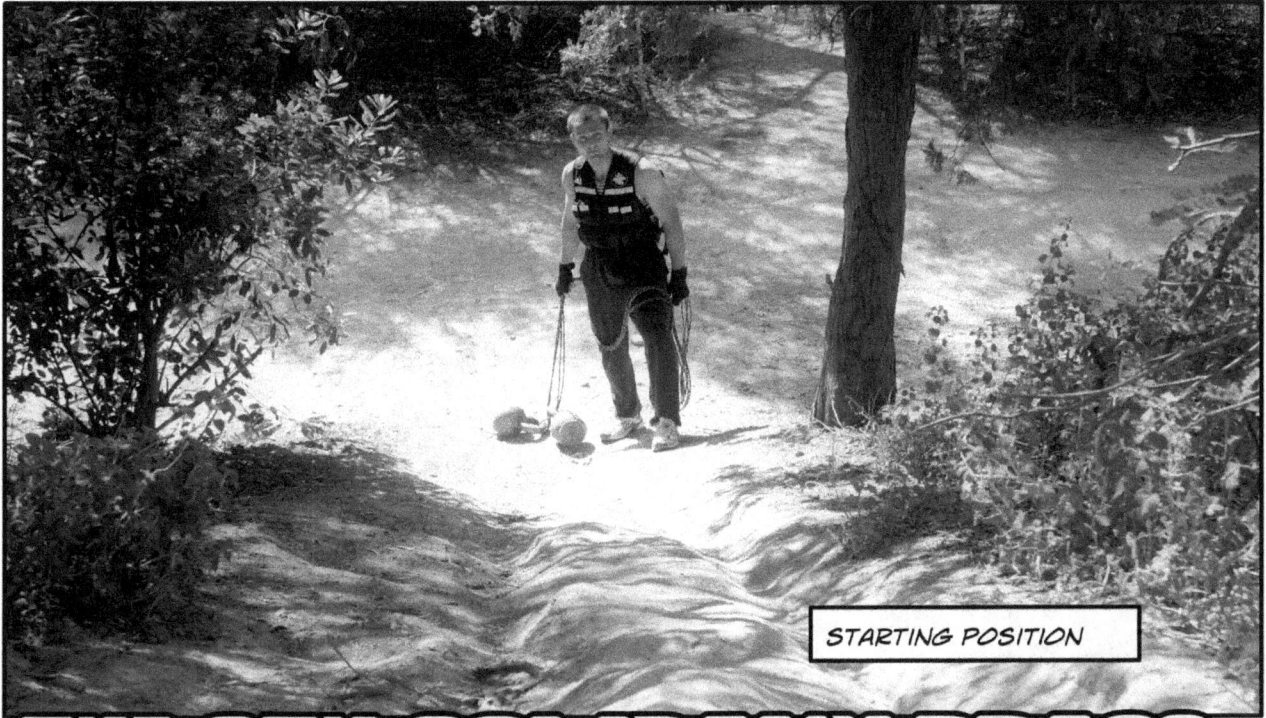

STARTING POSITION

THE 9TH COMPANY DRAGS

THIS SHOULD LITERALLY BE ONE OF THE HARDEST THINGS YOU HAVE EVER DONE. IF IT'S EASY, YOU NEED MORE WEIGHT.

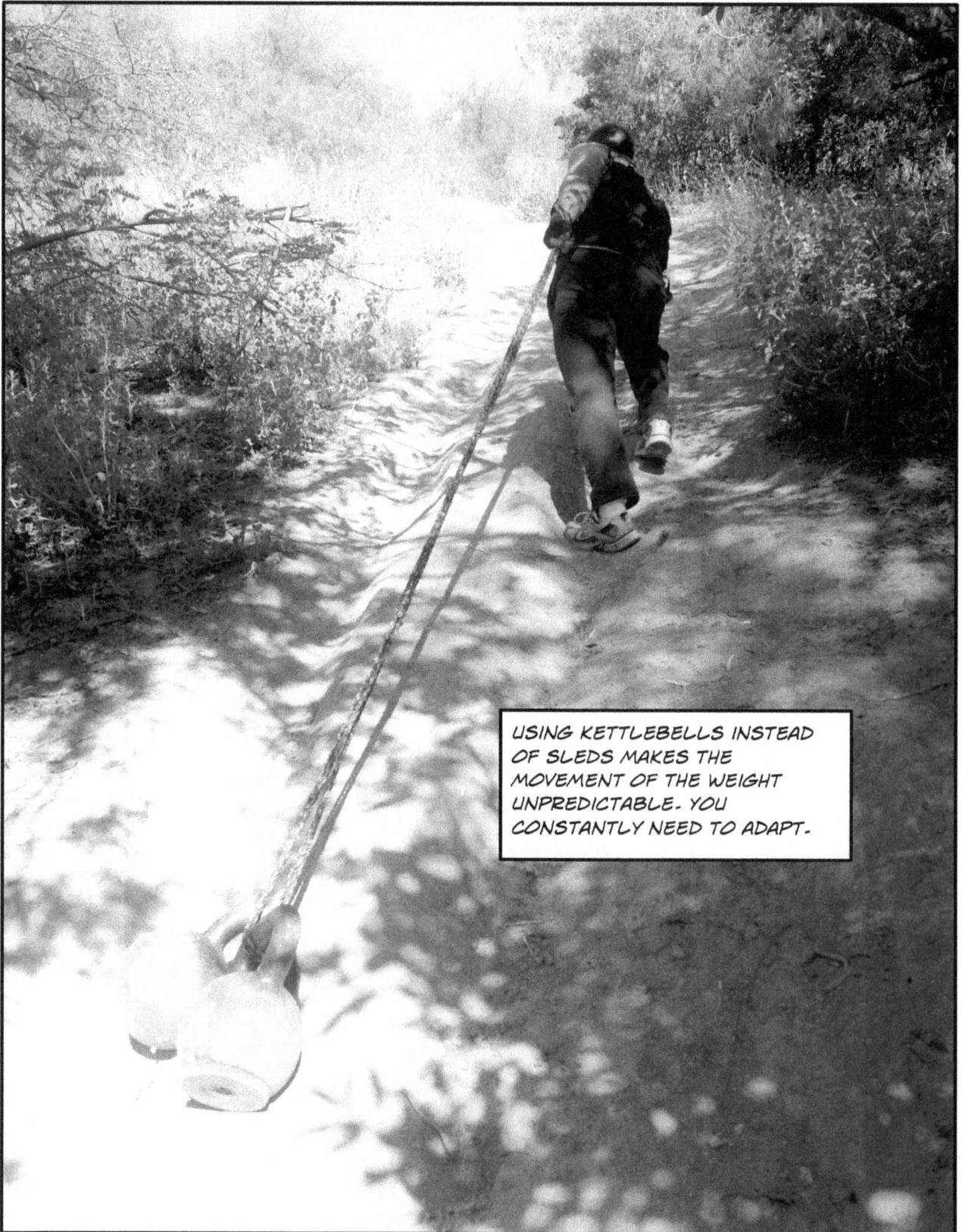

USING KETTLEBELLS INSTEAD OF SLEDS MAKES THE MOVEMENT OF THE WEIGHT UNPREDICTABLE. YOU CONSTANTLY NEED TO ADAPT.

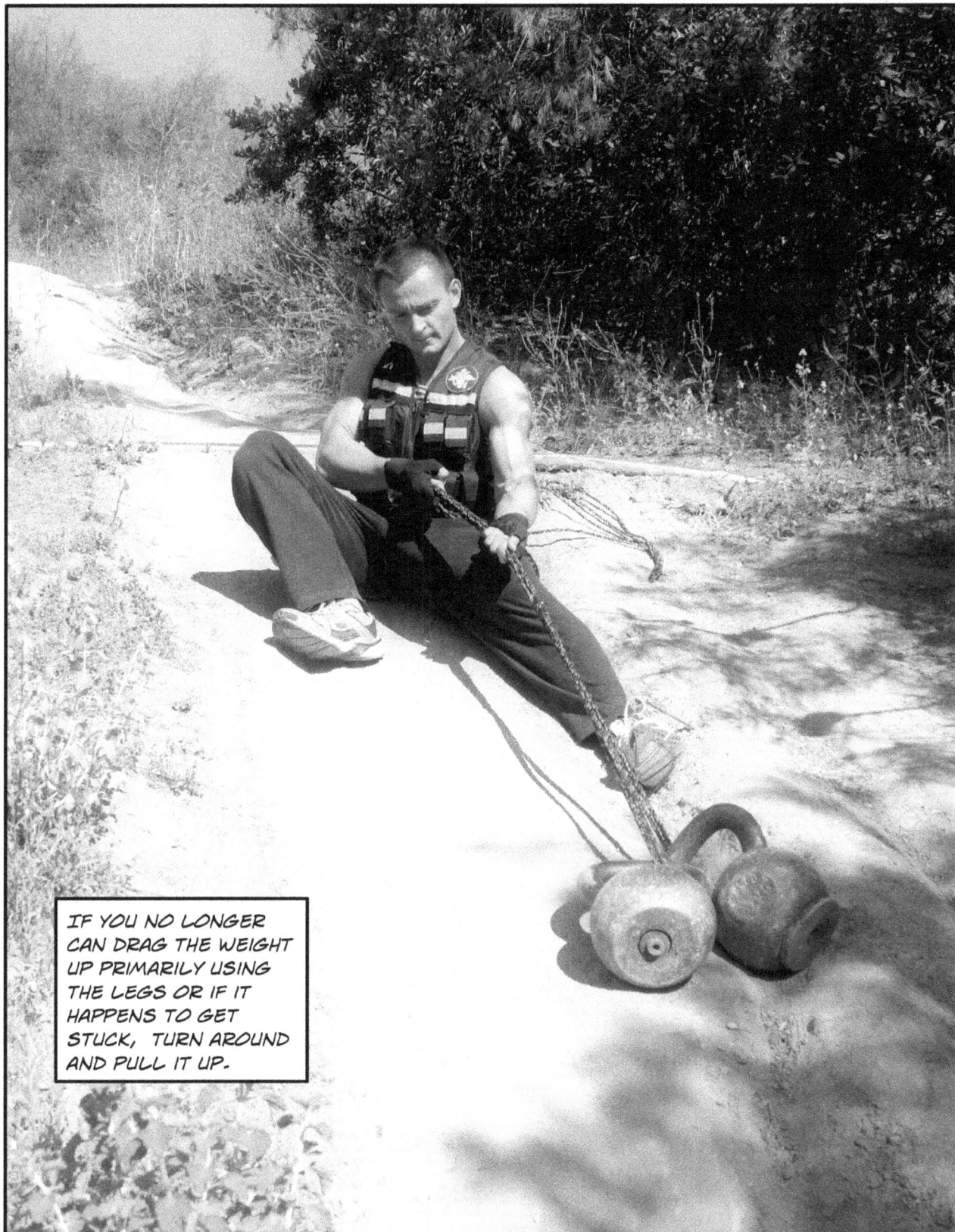

IF YOU NO LONGER CAN DRAG THE WEIGHT UP PRIMARILY USING THE LEGS OR IF IT HAPPENS TO GET STUCK, TURN AROUND AND PULL IT UP.

Please Comrades use common sense. Unless you are in excellent shape, these exercises are not for you. These exercises are difficult and may be dangerous if you throw caution to the wind. However, if unorthodox training floats your boat and you are training hard to crush Spartans and other enemies, then more power to your party. Train safe, stay hydrated, warm up, stretch, and always let others know where you are if you train alone.

IN SOVIET RUSSIA WE EAT SPARTANS FOR BREAKFAST

Chapter 19 - The Bear, Wolf, Rabbit, Beaver Connection

It is a well-known fact that some Comrades become easily bored. This chapter outlines basic options for weekly training variety. **(Note)** Chapter 19 focuses on four different training philosophies. Each training approach is one week long. Combining the four philosophies together equates to approximately one month of training.

Week 1

The Bear —Powerlifter

Week2

The Rabbit – Endurance athlete

Week 3

The Wolf - Bodybuilder

Week 4

The Beaver – Spetznaz Comrade Training

Week 1

The Bear -Powerlifter
The approach to week one power training is to lift 3 to 4 days max and lift heavy.
(Note) No need to get fancy, just standard heavy weight lifts with proper technique.

1) Deadlifts 3-4 sets 3-6 repetitions
2) Bench press 3-4 sets 3-6 repetitions
3) Squats 3-4 sets 3-6 repetitions (Standard squats / not Soviet squats)

Monday) Off
Tuesday) Power lifting
Wednesday) Off
Thursday) Power lifting
Friday) Off
Saturday) Power lifting
Sunday) Off

Comrades can incorporate other power exercises into the routine. However, if truly lifting heavy, the 3 exercises recommended above are more than enough. Develop strength and power in week 1. Try to keep a clean diet, however, it's not necessary in week one to be on the clean food patrol. Allow room for (3-4) cheat meals in week 1. Be sure to take the seventh day, (Sunday) off from lifting, but maintain a clean diet that day in preparation for week 2 endurance training.

Week 2
The Rabbit – Endurance athlete

Lots of Running Comrade! I know it's your favorite!
Got abbs?
No?
Ok then run!

Running = Awesomeness abdominals

Week one you were developing strength and power, week two you trim the fat and run! During this week be sure to stay hydrated and do not miss the Yugo Fuel breakfast every morning no matter what. Fuel up for every breakfast and get those Complex carbs in the system.

No fuel = body / mind crash

The Comrade must run no less than five days in the second week while keeping a clean diet. In week 2, allow yourself (1-2) cheat meals.

(Note) In Soviet Russia, we like to do a stanardish 4-8 mile daily run. It's a good idea to plan the run ahead of time. You can even use the internet spy maps provided by glorious satellites up in space to map and measure the runs.

Beginner

Monday) A slow run of 2-3 miles
Tuesday) A slow run of 3-6 miles
Wednesday) A slow run of 3 miles
Thursday) A slow run of 7 miles
Friday) Off
Saturday) A slow run of 10 miles
Sunday) Off

Warrior

Monday) A slow run of 3-5 miles
Tuesday) A slow run of 4-7 miles
Wednesday) A slow run of 3 miles
Thursday) A slow run of 7 miles
Friday) Off
Saturday) A slow run of 15 miles
Sunday) Off

Hero of the Soviet Russia

Monday) A slow run of 5-8 miles
Tuesday) A slow run of 6-10 miles
Wednesday) A slow run of 3 miles
Thursday) A slow run of 10 miles
Friday) Off
Saturday) A slow run of 20 miles
Sunday) Off

Week 3
The Wolf - Bodybuilder
In Week 3, stay with: 8-12 repetitions per set / 3-5 sets per exercise / 4-5 different exercises per session.
After each training session, incorporate some slow standard cardio of choice for no less than 30 minutes.

Beginer

Monday) Chest and 40 minutes of slow cardio
Tuesday) Back and 40 minutes of slow cardio
Wednesday) Legs (hams and thighs) / (cardio is optional on leg day)
Thursday) Off
Friday) Arms, abbs, calves and 60 minutes of slow cardio
Saturday) Shoulders and 60 minutes of slow cardio
Sunday) Off

Warrior

Monday) Chest and back / 40 minutes of slow cardio
Tuesday) Arms ,shoulders, abbs / 40 minutes of slow cardio
Wednesday) Legs (hams and thighs), calves (cardio is optional on leg day)
Thursday) Chest and back / 40 minutes of slow cardio
Friday) Arms, shoulders, abbs / 40 minutes of slow cardio
Saturday) Legs (hams and thighs), calves (cardio is optional on leg day)
Sunday) Off

Hero of Soviet Russia

Monday) Lower and middle-chest, lower and middle back, abbs, calves / 40 minutes of slow cardio
Tuesday) Biceps, shoulders, abbs / 40 minutes of slow cardio
Wednesday) Legs (hams and thighs) , calves, abbs (cardio is optional on leg day)
Thursday) Upper-chest, upper back, abbs, calves / 40 minutes of slow cardio
Friday) Triceps, shoulders, abbs / 40 minutes of slow cardio
Saturday) Legs (hams and thighs), calves (cardio is optional on leg day)
Sunday) Off

Week 4
The Beaver – Spetznaz Comrade Training
When it comes to the beaver, the training allows for options. Unlike the bear, wolf or rabbit, the beaver training states "The Comrade must pick any exercise he or she likes from chapter 18 and try his best to fall through on that exercise".
(Note) After the workout, (but only after the workout and not any other time), the Comrade may claim reward to a glorious cheat meal.

Beginner

Monday) Off
Tuesday) Spetznaz Comrade Training (exercise of choice)
Wednesday) Off
Thursday) Spetznaz Comrade Training (exercise of choice)
Friday) Off
Saturday) Spetznaz Comrade Training (exercise of choice)
Sunday) Off

Warrior

Monday) Spetznaz Comrade Training (exercise of choice)
Tuesday) Spetznaz Comrade Training (exercise of choice)
Wednesday) Off
Thursday) Spetznaz Comrade Training (exercise of choice)
Friday) Off
Saturday) Spetznaz Comrade Training (exercise of choice)
Sunday) Off

Hero of Soviet Russia

Monday) Spetznaz Comrade Training (exercise of choice)
Tuesday) Spetznaz Comrade Training (exercise of choice)
Wednesday) Spetznaz Comrade Training (exercise of choice)
Thursday) Spetznaz Comrade Training (exercise of choice)
Friday) Off
Saturday) Spetznaz Comrade Training (exercise of choice)
Sunday) Off

NO MORE RESOLUTIONS, ONLY COMMITMENT.

Chapter 20 – Words of Glorious Wisdom

Attitude- Without the right attitude, it is almost impossible to achieve any serious fitness goal. If you want to get Russian Ripped, stay positive!

Consistency- Getting Russian Ripped takes time. Every week you must maintain consistency to take steps in the right direction. Inconsistency does not allow for a proper habit to develop. Bad, inconsistent training habits = Bad, inconsistent results.

Procrastination- Kicking the can down the road solves nothing. As a matter of fact, when it comes to health, "I will do it tomorrow" only makes things worse. Take responsibility and start now. Tomorrow is always tomorrow, but one day tomorrow will not come. Move your @$$ today.

Priorities- In life, we all have certain serious obligations to which we are committed. Becoming Russian Ripped also requires a serious commitment. If commitment to training is not one of the top five priorities on the long term to do list, you are fooling yourself. Is getting in shape a top priority for you?

Focus- What you focus on and think about most is the direction in which you go.
This applies to getting in shape and almost everything else. No focus = No direction.

Wishful thinking vs Action- Many Comrades talk about weight loss and think that one day it will magically happen. Thinking about weight loss and training for weight loss are two very different things. One works, the other one does not.

Starting Stage- Everyone starts at a different fitness level. The important thing is that you move forward and do not compare yourself to anyone else. "You, get in shape for you."

Friends and Family- Often friends and family do not understand how difficult things may be for a Comrade when he or she is trying to drop a significant amount of weight. It might be a good idea to tell those close to you that you made a decision to change, and you would highly appreciate it if they did not offer you junk food or other non-healthy foods. Sometimes, Comrades are assholes, and they will do it just to piss you off, to test you, out of jealousy or stupidity. It is in those moments you must find the strength within yourself to overcome the BS. By conquering yourself from within and passing on non-healthy sugary fat foods you develop a healthy habit. The more often you say NO to unhealthy choices, the stronger you become. With enough No's under the belt you will not be fazed regardless of circumstances. It becomes a way of life, not a quick fix infomercial that makes you feel good for ten minutes at a time.

(Note) When a Comrade excels in weight loss, (friends, family, acquaintances and coworkers) have a tendency to reacts in one of two ways.
1) They feel left out or insecure on the inside so they might try to bring you down.
2) They jump on the band wagon and follow your lead.

Sprinter weight loss mentality vs marathon weight loss mentality
Most Comrades want things now damn it! They think like sprinters and so they do not go the distance. They burn out. The sooner the Comrade who is trying to lose weight realizes that a quarter pound or a tenth of a pound lost every week is significant progress the better. Weight loss sprinters drop weight fast and gain it back fast too. Weight loss marathon runners go slowly, maintain focus, remain consistent and cross that finish line without a burnout.

Physical pain- Is part of the process. But when significant changes start to happen, pain no longer remains a major factor.

Why so many Comrades fail? Some of the reasons are:
- Negative attitude
- Lack of commitment
- Lack of priority
- Lack of organization
- Procrastination
- The changes do not happen quickly
- Unrealistic short term goals
- Lack of focus
- Vague goals are set instead of clear goals
- Peer pressure
- Rewarding oneself often and not training hard enough (yo-yoing)

Bottom line Comrade is that getting in shape is achievable for most Comrades as long as the Comrades don't lie to themselves, push themselves and accept responsibility. Many of us have busy lives with little room for change. But the truth is you don't have to hit the ground running like a mad man. Starting as a turtle and being consistent is still a step forward. Moving slow is better than not moving at all. Believe in yourself and don't let anyone ever bring you down. To achieve the image or fitness level you are striving for is in your hands. Stay strong Comrade, move forward and never give up. Thank you.

Say your name…..**You are a winner.**
Say your name…..**You are strong.**
Say your name…..**You are motivated.**
Say your name…..**You are positive.**
Say your name…..**You are organized.**
Say your name…..**You make positive plans and fall through on them.**
Say your name…..**You take responsibility for your actions.**

It is only **(The End)** when you choose to end it.

ABOUT THE AUTHOR

Ilya Sulima is a real Russian Comrade. He now resides in an amazing place called California USA. He was certified by multiple personal training organizations and has been working as a personal trainer since 2004 . Ilya worked as a trainer for 24 Hour Fitness, LA Fitness, Bally Total Fitness and other fitness companies. He competed in bodybuilding and holds a black belt in karate.

www.ingramcontent.com/pod-product-compliance
Lightning Source LLC
Chambersburg PA
CBHW080659110426
42739CB00034B/3331

* 9 7 8 0 6 1 5 6 9 3 5 9 0 *